Pilgrimage

Text copyright © Andrew Jones 2011
The author asserts the moral right
to be identified as the author of this work

Published by
The Bible Reading Fellowship
15 The Chambers, Vineyard
Abingdon OX14 3FE
United Kingdom
Tel: +44 (0)1865 319700
Email: enquiries@brf.org.uk
Website: www.brf.org.uk
BRF is a Registered Charity

ISBN 978 1 84101 834 8
First published 2011
10 9 8 7 6 5 4 3 2 1 0
All rights reserved

Acknowledgments
Unless otherwise stated, scripture quotations are taken from The Jerusalem Bible © 1966 by
Darton, Longman & Todd Ltd and Doubleday & Company, Inc.

Scripture quotations taken from The New Revised Standard Version of the Bible, Anglicised
Edition, copyright © 1989, 1995 by the Division of Christian Education of the National
Council of the Churches of Christ in the United States of America, are used by permission.
All rights reserved.

Psalm quotations are taken from The Revised Psalter, © 1966, copyright assigned to the
Archbishops' Council.

Extract from 'The Twelve Days of Christmas 2009' copyright © 2009 Carol Ann Duffy.
Reproduced by permission of the author c/o Rogers, Coleridge & White Ltd, 20 Powis Mews,
London W11 1JN.

Some of the material in Chapter 6 has been previously published in *Quiet Spaces: Tomorrow*,
ed. Heather Fenton (BRF, 2011).

A catalogue record for this book is available from the British Library

Printed in Singapore by Craft Print International Ltd

Pilgrimage

The journey to remembering our story

ANDREW JONES

In memory of my wonderful parents,
Tom and Kathleen;
they were the first to set me on the pilgrim's way

ACKNOWLEDGMENTS

Many people have enabled this book to be written. I am grateful to those eight people who accompanied me to the various pilgrimage places and, although disguised, for their permission to use some of the experiences they shared with me as we travelled together.

I would also like to thank the family and the estate of the late Simon Bailey for giving me permission to publish the liturgy that we used together on Bardsey Island.

There have also been a number of people whose patience I have appreciated during the writing of this book, especially those who live alongside me in the four churches that I serve. They have taught me a great deal about the more general pilgrimage of life that happens naturally from day to day.

I have valued the conversations that I have had with various friends and colleagues, especially Fraser, Sue, Leslie, Michael, Evelyn, Verena and Jim. And I am grateful for the support and encouragement offered by Bishop Andy and for Naomi Starkey's original idea and constant inspiration, without which this book would never have happened.

CONTENTS

✳

FOREWORD

'How can we sing the Lord's song in a strange land?' That was
a question asked by an exile more than 2000 years ago. It's a
question many are asking today as they contemplate a sense of
isolation and alienation from cherished and inherited patterns
of faith and belief. In this book, Andrew Jones seeks to address
the contemporary experience of exile with the ancient practice
of pilgrimage. Pilgrimage: the journey to remembering our story
describes the biblical event of the exile and its significance for
those affected—the remnant in Jerusalem and those taken to a
foreign land whose songs we know well from the psalms. This
event generated decisive changes in the structure, faith and life of
the Hebrew people, and led, among other things, to the formation
of the Hebrew text that Christians call the Old Testament.

The exile has become a powerful metaphor for Christians and
Jews alike, allowing them to describe their own situations and
suggest new ways of understanding their history and where God
might lead them into his future. One of the ways in which we
can respond to this exilic sense of alienation and powerlessness
is to discover the presence of God journeying with us. The Bible
is replete with stories of travel and how our very lives are rightly
seen as a pilgrimage towards that place where we will see Christ
face to face. Andrew draws the threads of this theology together by
describing how lives, sometimes characterised by hopelessness and
despair, are transformed by the physical and spiritual journeys they
undertake. We are treated to a rich array of sacred places, shrines
and holy sites across four countries. The stories are personal and
moving, showing Andrew's own experience of pastoral ministry
for over 25 years. In each of them we see the importance of place

but, more importantly, of encounter with Christ. If the psalmist's question resonates down the ages, this book provides us with a hopeful, profound and exciting way of answering it today.

The Right Reverend Andrew John
Bishop of Bangor

✳

INTRODUCTION

It was a Friday lunchtime and I was visiting some of my parishioners in the local hospital. After several bedside visits, I went, as
I normally do, to the hospital chapel to say prayers for those I'd
met. As it happens, it's no longer a chapel in the strict sense of
that word but a worship centre for all religious faiths—and on this
Friday lunchtime it was so full that I couldn't even get close to it.
Why? Because of the impressively lengthy queue of Muslims waiting
to go in and say their midday prayers. I later mentioned this to the
Anglican chaplain and he told me that he's lucky to get four people
for Holy Communion on a Sunday. While the Muslim commitment
to regular prayer impresses me, it also causes me concern when
I compare it to the way the traditional Christian culture treats
prayer as an optional extra. I have been convinced for a long time
that it is precisely this serious lack of deep commitment that serves
as the major cause of forgetting the Christian story.

The place where I serve as a priest is a popular holiday resort
with a historic and beautiful church that is an attractive place for
weddings—especially for people who live elsewhere and, as many
do, have a second home in the parish. Increasingly, when I begin
to plan a wedding with a couple, I find that they have fewer ideas
about hymns, less and less opinion regarding choice of prayers
or Bible readings and—I have to say—apparently little genuine
interest in the religious side of the forthcoming ceremony. In fact,
nowadays, booking the church for the service tends to come second
to booking the hotel for the reception. On the day of the service,
fewer and fewer people sing the hymns and hardly anyone seems
to know the Lord's Prayer. Far too often, the couple seem more
concerned about being married 'in the sight of this congregation'
than 'in the sight of God'. Sadly, for many couples getting married,

it's not a matter of having forgotten the Christian story but, rather, of not knowing the story at all.

As well as at weddings (and the same is true for funerals and baptisms), I have noticed a shift in religious awareness when I go to schools to talk to children about the Christian faith: it's like talking a foreign language. Of course, I always receive a warm welcome from the staff and the children and we always have great fun together. But when it comes to talking about God, I realise only too quickly how marginal the church has become to the lives of most people. Parents are generally concerned about children doing well in school and behaving in an acceptable way, but passing on the Christian story is no longer a priority. After more than 25 years in pastoral ministry, one of my greatest concerns is that, as the Christian church in the developed world, we may be on the verge of forgetting altogether 'the story' of God's creating and redeeming work in history.

Although a fair bit of the opening part of this book is about an exile that happened in Jerusalem and Babylon during the sixth century BC, it is not actually a book about that particular exile; nor is it a book on the Old Testament. It's a book about the Christian experience of pilgrimage. I want to show how the experience of journeying together can help us never to forget 'our story'—sharing the narrative of the Christian faith which tells us who we are, where we have come from and where we are going. It was, however, the American Old Testament scholar Walter Brueggemann who first encouraged me (and continues to encourage me) to recognise the significance of that sixth-century BC exile in the endeavour to rescue our story. First, that particular exile was a crucial theological experience in which real people went through a particular chain of events that not only changed their lives radically but also changed the whole structure of their religious thinking. Second, it not only serves as a metaphor for understanding and interpreting people's experience of God today, but can deepen our sense of participation in God's ongoing work of creation.

Since I discovered what Brueggemann had to say about exile and realised the value of using some of the experiences of that exile to make some sense of where we have come to as a church today, I have found that the most effective place to work through all of this is in the practice of pilgrimage. I have led pilgrimages in many different places with many different groups of people, and I have found that this ancient practice has the power to awaken believers at all stages of faith to the urgent need to 'remember the story'— and the theme of exile plays a vital role in that awakening. It is interesting to note that the one activity that almost every religious tradition has in common is pilgrimage. Muslims go to Mecca, Jews go to Jerusalem, Hindus to the Ganges, Buddhists to the Himalayas, and we Christians have developed a vast network of important pilgrimage sites all over the world. It is also noteworthy that this network of pilgrim places, large and small, increasingly draws significant numbers of visitors, and their experience of renewal and refreshment of faith at those places often far outweighs what is happening in many churches. Both pilgrimage and pilgrim places have much to teach the contemporary church, and bring many challenges to it.

Consequently, three crucial threads run through the whole of this book. First, I retell the story of the experience of exile that took place in Jerusalem and Babylon between 597 and 539BC. I make no apology for doing so, for, in order to achieve what I want to achieve in this book, I believe strongly that a proper understanding of the historical events of the exile is essential. Second, I want to draw parallels between what happened then and some of what is happening now, both in the Church and in the developed world generally. In many different ways, the Church is in an exile situation today. One of the main thrusts of the opening chapters will be to identify some key moments in the Babylonian exile and to draw from them some basis for reflection on what is happening to God's children today. Third, just as the Jewish exiles were freed to return home in 539BC, so we in the Church can be encouraged to seek new ways that lead to freedom from the chains of our own exile situation. In the final part of this book, I will show how the age-old practice of pilgrimage offers us a life-transforming way out of our contemporary exile and points us to the way home—the place where true commitment to the story of God's creating and redeeming work helps us to live an authentic and balanced life. Finally I will reflect further on what I mean by 'freedom' and 'going home' by focusing on eight popular places of pilgrimage—two in Wales, two in Ireland, two in Scotland and two in England. We 'visit' the eight in a particular sequence, which links to the themes that have emerged over the course of this book, bringing together the experiences of the sixth-century BC exiles and 21st-century Christian pilgrims.

Part 1

*By the waters of Babylon we sat down and wept
when we remembered Zion.*

PSALM 137:1

To get to the heart of what the Bible is all about, one of the metaphors that I most enjoy using is that of a 'door'. A door usually leads us into different places and offers new opportunities and fresh encounters. The door as a metaphor for understanding the Bible leads us into a place of encounter with two of the great monotheistic faiths of the world, Judaism and Christianity. A door also needs hinges to hold it in place, and the Bible has four such hinges: Exodus, Exile, Incarnation and Resurrection. Of the four, the exile is probably the least well oiled of those hinges but it is as definitive as any of the others to Jews and Christians seeking to understand fully what it means to be a child of God.

SETTING THE SCENE

The exile is something that happened to the Jews in the mid-sixth century BC. For all sorts of different reasons, the king of Babylon conquered Jerusalem, destroyed the temple and took a vast number of the population as prisoners, keeping them in Babylon for the best part of 50 years. As such, along with the exodus, the exile is probably one of the two most definitive experiences in the whole of the Old Testament. But far too many historians of the exile have assumed that the connection between exile and exodus is more theological and symbolical than historical—exodus symbolising 'deliverance', and the return from exile symbolising a 'restoration' of that previous deliverance, thus relegating exile to second-division status. If those historians are right, then the exodus is predominantly the experience of a dispossessed and powerless people moving to a place of possession and empowerment, while the return from exile is the completion of a divine relationship between God and his children that started with exodus. The exile was a stretching and a breaking of the relationship created at the exodus, and it was actually the return home from exile that served as the restoration.

If we see exile simply as a different setting for a more powerful exodus theology, we lose sight of the fact that exile can be a metaphor that points to a radically different approach to understanding and interpreting the relationship between God and his children. Both in exile and on their return from exile, the Jewish people experienced what it was like to live in a minority in the midst of a people they could neither control nor escape from. The exile is the story of a people in a situation of utter powerlessness and vulnerability; despite that, however, they were still a people with a story of their own. Their experience of dehumanisation, devaluation and exploitation added sharpness and focus to their story and made them appreciate its importance more than they had ever done before.

EXILE IN RELATION TO EXODUS, INCARNATION AND RESURRECTION

Exodus, Exile, Incarnation and Resurrection stand, then, as the four great moments that call forth the most creative theological reflection both on God's activity in the world and on the nature of the community of God's children. Indeed, the social contexts surrounding all four of these biblical 'hinges' speak to different aspects of the contemporary church's situation. However, I am convinced that the exile, above all, can be an exciting metaphor for interpreting the church in today's world, a time (as the Old Testament exile was) of trying to live by an alternative set of values among many competing powers and authorities. It can suggest endless creative possibilities for those who continue to find themselves strangers in a strange land—a land on the verge of forgetting how to 'sing the Lord's song' (Psalm 137:4), a people living in 'Babylon' and far from 'home'.

Jews have used the exile as a defining experience for their faith, life and self-understanding, and some scholars suggest that even the later New Testament continuation of the story of God's people is set in a framework of exile: they were a powerless minority community in the midst of the mighty Roman empire. From the time when Abraham first journeyed from his place of familiarity into a foreign land, the people of God have been on the move, and often to places and situations of exile. However, I will use the theme of exile with specific reference to the events between 597 and 539BC, described in the books of the prophets Isaiah, Jeremiah and Ezekiel. In fact, about a third of the Old Testament is in some way connected with this historical period.

If Exodus is the beginning of the story and Incarnation and Resurrection together form the Christian climax of the story, then a proper understanding of Exile in this restricted sense—as the middle bit of the story—is crucial. It is a time in which we see the Jews moving swiftly from one emotion to another. Throughout the literature that emerges out of the exile, the Jews are a people who wait, who anticipate, who are warned, who experience, who reflect, and who then return home, where they are able to start to make sense of the whole process. The act of remembering helped the Jews come to terms with what had happened, and their determination to keep telling their own story ensured that the period during and after the exile became one of the most creative periods in their history.

Obviously, exile is neither an easy nor a straightforward metaphor. To use the history of the exile as a metaphor means digging deeply into its traditions and drawing from them events that reflect our present situation or that help us see the present in new and different ways. This is why it is crucial to see beyond the geography of the sixth-century exile and reflect on it as a metaphor of culture, society, spirituality and worship: it touches every aspect of life. By going back to read what happened in Jerusalem and Babylon just over 2500 years ago, we can start to see our own dire situation in the light of God's everlasting promises and God's unchanging faithfulness.

＊

Chapter 1

THE EXILE OF GOD'S CHILDREN

In this chapter I will simply retell the story of the exile. There is so much that we could say about it, but I will include only those parts of the story that are relevant to our later exploration of the exile as a metaphor for understanding our own situation in terms of both church and contemporary culture.

BABYLON CONQUERS JERUSALEM

Babylonian interest in Israel had been brewing for quite some time. In 605BC, under the shrewd leadership of King Nebuchadnezzar, the Babylonians defeated the Egyptians at the battle of Carchemish, and, a year later, headed for Syria and Israel. The prophets of the period saw the hand of God in what had happened. Jeremiah declared the impending downfall of Jerusalem (chs. 4 and 5) and in 597BC Nebuchadnezzar struck his first blow on Israel, although it took him ten years to achieve a final victory. By 587BC Jerusalem was destroyed, its temple in ruins, the surrounding land devastated and a significant number of its people taken as prisoners to Babylon. It was a cataclysmic experience that called into question all that had previously given the people meaning, value and purpose in life. They were left searching for God in what was now for them a strange place, both physically and metaphorically.

THOSE LEFT BEHIND

Not all the people of Jerusalem were taken into captivity. Throughout the book of Lamentations we read of the desperate conditions of those who were left behind. Not only were they exploited by neighbouring peoples but they were sunk in despair as they gathered around the ruined temple in their holy city. The destruction of the temple was a severe blow for many different reasons, not least because the Jews believed that God, in a profoundly supernatural way, dwelt in the temple. At that time it would have been natural for many to claim that God's 'heavenly dwelling' and their national 'shrine' (the temple) were in some way mysteriously and intimately related (see Psalms 122; 132; 135). This belief provided them with a sense of the protective presence of God maintaining their national way of life and well-being. Theologically, we could describe it as a concept of 'real presence', which is not, however, to be confused with a 'tied presence'. For the Jews, God was not tied to the temple; rather, his presence was real in the temple, just as, in the Catholic tradition of the Eucharist, Christ's presence is understood to be real but not tied exclusively to the particular elements of bread and wine. But the destruction of the temple building played havoc with the subtlety of this distinction between 'real' and 'tied'. Now, both the exiles and those who remained in Jerusalem had to begin the painful process of comprehending what it meant to be geographically separated from God, whether by distance or by destruction.

The prophet Jeremiah refers to those left behind as 'the poor people of the land' (39:10) but he states that they were actually given vineyards and fields, which probably once belonged to those who had been exiled to Babylon as exiles. There is historical evidence to show that they were not simply the 'dregs' of society, as is sometimes held. Clearly they were able to produce a substantial theological assessment of what had happened and how it would affect the development of both their faith and their culture. One of their key collections was the book of Lamentations. They would also have continued to worship together and sought to remember their particular interpretation of what had happened and aspects of their tradition that they judged worthy of preservation. But on the whole, physical survival under difficult conditions was far more urgent than spending time in theological reflection. Such reflection, in fact, became the urgent priority of the exiles rather than of those left behind. The Babylonian exiles, in their desperation, felt it essential to engage in this task in order to preserve their identity, protect their traditions and find ways of retelling the story, lest they forget.

CONDITIONS IN BABYLON

Scholarly opinions differ as to the conditions imposed upon the exiles while they were in Babylon, especially as time passed. One opinion is that it was a hard slog. From a socio-political point of view, captivity and resettlement as a permanent minority on foreign soil meant a significant loss of power as well as the loss of their symbols of religious and cultural identity. For the exiles, as for those left behind, the temple in Jerusalem had been a tangible symbol of God's real presence among his people and of God's continual participation in their journey of life. Its destruction meant that God could no longer be relied upon as a travelling companion, as he had been on the people's wilderness journey after the exodus. The Jews became muddled as to why this devastation could ever have happened. Was God angry with them? Had he been defeated by another, more powerful god? Was the exile God's judgment on Jewish arrogance? Could it have possibly been his curse on their unfaithfulness? Or was he impatient about the growing injustices in the land? Or was it all politics and nothing to do with God at all?

Not only the book of Lamentations but also the prophecies of

Jeremiah, Ezekiel and Isaiah, as well as some of the Psalms (Psalms 22; 26; 30; 32), show how preoccupied the people were with trying to find reasons for the catastrophe. At the same time, the writings of the period are united in their double conviction that while God's love had not evaporated, the covenant between God and his people had been severely damaged by their waywardness. This was nothing short of a serious crisis of faith, and the writer of Psalm 137 offers perhaps the best theological reflection on the nature of that crisis. The psalm is a community lament with a poignant opening but it soon moves on to express hatred and longing for revenge. It presents a mixture of emotions—homesickness, regret, sadness, melancholy, anger and vengeance.

At the beginning of the psalm, we hear deep mourning in Babylon and great indignation at the way in which the Babylonians had violated the exiled people's most sacred religious and patriotic feelings. In the face of this, the people are wrathful, and we read one of the most vengeful parts of the whole Psalter: by verse 9 the exiles have worked themselves up to a blind hate and a frenzied rage that they can no longer restrain. Scholars tell us that atrocities such as those recorded in verse 9 did occur in the ancient Near East (Isaiah 13:16; Hosea 13:16) and the psalmist hopes that the people will have the opportunity for revenge.

Historically, this was more of a call for justice than for spite. Jews at that time had no real ideal of love for enemies; nor had they worked out a concept of divine punishment after death. For them, if God's justice was to be done, then it must be done immediately, in the here and now. The psalm addresses the pain of life; as for so many people today, that pain spawns a frightening awareness of the hatred that many people feel, and also the sense of despair and hopelessness that the hatred brings with it. Whatever the precise historical details of the psalm, it certainly suggests that the exiles could no longer sing the old familiar songs that they had enjoyed in the temple precincts. In the face of this devastation, the majority of the Jews are speechless—at least for the moment.

While accepting that the exile was a fundamentally life-shattering experience, some scholars would argue that, as time passed, life for the captives was not all that bad. Some evidence suggests that, on arrival in Babylon, they were not dispersed and forced to leave loved ones; rather, they were allowed to remain in relatively large groups and were located in previously ruined cities. The suggestion is that they were able, if not encouraged, to rebuild those places and achieve an element of independent social organisation; many even aspired to political influence. The prophet Jeremiah recommends building homes and tilling the land (29:5). Indeed, Ezra claims that when they were eventually allowed to return to Jerusalem at the end of the exile, some returned as wealthy people, even with slaves of their own (2:64–66). If this was the case, then soon after the major deportations, 'exile' for many did not mean simply captivity but possibly prosperity. We get the impression that a Babylonian Jewish population was allowed to develop and that the Babylonian authorities looked favourably on such a development. Clearly, for some, the Babylonian life was good and they succumbed to its many temptations quite readily.

WORSHIPPING GOD IN BABYLON

Not a great deal of information remains available to describe with confidence the precise nature of the exiles' life of worship in Babylon. Some say that this could well have been the time and place when the synagogue developed fully as a house of worship and a place of learning, but, again, this is not entirely clear. Undoubtedly new ways of worshipping God must have emerged in the light of the dramatically changed circumstances. What we already know about the faith of the Jewish people in the days before the exile makes it almost impossible to believe that they would have even thought of withdrawing from worship—even without a temple. In the book of Ezekiel, a group of 'elders' approach the prophet, seeking advice, possibly on worship (8:1; 14:1; 20:1). It has even been suggested that they wanted to know whether they should commence on a building programme for a new temple in Babylon. It is also assumed that the exile was the context for a reiteration of the solemn importance of observing the sabbath and circumcision as purely religious (rather than partly cultural) acts. With the loss of holy place (the Jerusalem temple), observing holy time (the sabbath) and holy marks (circumcision) gained much more prominence.

This holy time and these holy marks focused mainly on the re-enforcement of faith traditions that already touched the lives of the exiles at various levels; they were not new things but they were given a new significance by the changed circumstances. Although much older than the exile, circumcision, for instance, now gained a much more highly charged importance: it became the holy mark that distinguished the Jews, and it remained a mark that the Babylonians could not see. Similarly, sabbath observance provided a new opportunity for the exiles to pause for a while in faith and remember their story, to retell it and to study how it had unfolded and continued to unfold.

Many scholars would argue that there was another interesting innovation in exile, namely the renewed emphasis on the idea of a temporary and more localised holy space as described in Deuteronomy—the wilderness tabernacle, which was intended to mark a place where the presence of God could be remembered and his presence called upon. Perhaps the most significant of the religious developments during the period of the exile, however, was the emergence of the idea of the text of scripture. Indeed, one of the fundamental legacies of this period was the people's determination to gather together all the old stories about God's activity in the world and his particular relationship with their nation. A great deal of the canon of the Old Testament was collected, collated and written down at this time, and, in order to deepen the relationship between the text and the people, three things were introduced in

Babylon. First, as previously mentioned, there was a development of the synagogue in order to house the text. Second, there was the introduction of study centres (in Hebrew, *Beth Midrash*) in order to provide a place to study the text. Third, the role of the rabbi was formalised into one of function rather than honour, in order to teach and interpret the text. From this time on, the text of scripture was to play an integral role in the worshipping life of the Jewish nation.

Circumcision, sabbath, synagogue, tabernacle and text were all serious attempts by the exiled people to receive again, to imagine again, to understand again and to practise again the presence of God in their midst. Although, on their return to Jerusalem, the construction of a new temple was started almost immediately, theologically it never quite matched the role that the previous temple of Solomon had played in the life of both individual and nation. In many ways, the prestige and theological importance of that original temple were now transferred to the reading, listening, teaching and interpretation of the text. Through the text, the people's story was retold and remembered and the lessons learnt in exile were cherished.

LIBERATION

By 539BC, everything had changed. Cyrus, king of Persia, captured Babylon and declared freedom to the Jews, even authorising the rebuilding of the temple (Ezra 1). The accounts of his victory suggest strongly that he regarded himself as a restorer of the religious traditions that had been lost, as well as the reconciler of peoples who had been divided. Indeed, many of the sources claim that the initiative for reconstituting the Jewish community in accordance with their own religious laws was an act of Persian generosity but also a political policy to create a passive empire which would inevitably benefit the wider Persian kingdom. The whole affair, from beginning to end, was steeped in the violent politics of the day.

Inevitably, the experience of returning home was to prove extremely difficult and, in fact, not all the Jews opted to go back. Some decided to remain in Babylon, either because they had intermarried and acquired new family connections or because they had simply grown accustomed to a new way of life. Some emigrated elsewhere: there was already a vibrant Jewish community in Elephantine on the upper Nile in Egypt. Both Isaiah and Jeremiah refer to the Jews living in Egypt (Isaiah 19:18; Jeremiah 24:8), so it is not unreasonable to think that some Babylonian-based Jews opted to head for Egypt to seek prosperity, rather than returning to face the ruins and poverty of Jerusalem.

The Jews living in exile in Babylon had come to see themselves as the 'remnant' who had saved both the religious and national traditions of orthodox Judaism. They were the ones who claimed to be the 'righteous Israel' (as opposed to those who had never left Jerusalem) and saw themselves as having the right to control temple, law and land on their return. For them, exile had been an experience of purification, preparing them for the new opportunity that lay ahead. Ezra (ch. 4) writes about the tensions between 'the people of the land' and 'the sons of exile', but, as with the various scholarly opinions regarding the actual conditions of exile, so opinions vary as to the degree of tension that existed between the returnees and those already in Jerusalem at the time of the great homecoming, more than 50 years after the main departure. Whatever the realities of return, and whatever the nature of the reunions with distant relatives and rediscovery of the land itself in the aftermath of exile, all Jews, whether exiles or those who had remained in Jerusalem, emerged from this cataclysmic experience with a renewed image of God, a renewed strategy for preserving identity and a renewed sense of hope in the midst of hopelessness.

✳

REMEMBERING THE STORY

For the Jews, the exile proved to be both a defining faith moment and an opportunity for rediscovering the roots of their faith. From a faith perspective, they learnt what it meant to be God's children in a context of despair and defeat, but at the same time they discovered a fresh faith, one that would sustain them for generations to come. Ironically, the exile proved to be a time of outstanding theological reflection, as the people were forced to reflect on where they had come from, what had happened to them and where they had ended up. Historically, politically, socially, culturally and in literary and spiritual terms, this was a time of both staggering change and amazing creativity. Significantly for us, what emerged from it emerged primarily in a context of profound threat to the very survival of the Jewish community and the Jewish religion. To live as they did for almost half a century as a cultural, political and religious minority in a hostile environment was hard. But in this catastrophe the exiles were forced to explore new ways of understanding God's working in the world and the nature of their own cooperative relationship with this active and busy God. In some ways, the whole experience of exile turned out to be a tremendous pilgrimage of renewal. At the end of this chapter we will consider further the fascinating relationship between exile and pilgrimage.

A TIME OF DEEP THINKING

As we have seen, a major part of that pilgrimage of renewal was the process of remembering and the subsequent collecting of the people's stories of faith, so that the bigger story of their covenant with God could be preserved for ever. It is a tribute to Israel's persistence and endurance that the story was not simply remembered and recorded but also deepened and enriched.

As a result of the exile, the prophets Jeremiah, Ezekiel and Isaiah encouraged the people to believe that they could worship God anywhere, not only in Jerusalem (Ezekiel 11:16). It was probably not long after, when the people began to realise that what the prophets were saying was in fact true, that they began meeting as small groups in each other's homes to reflect on this development of doctrine, to be instructed in the scriptural tradition that backed the development, and to worship together. This 'gathering together' is the original meaning of the Hebrew word 'synagogue' and it is here that we find the process beginning of gathering together a substantial part of what would eventually become the Old Testament. Fortunately, there were priests in their midst who either knew the stories by heart or had managed to bring some of the sacred writings with them. It was not so much that the exiles sat down and consciously 'wrote scripture' but more a matter of small groups of people dealing with issues and answering questions that were raised by the context of exile. The story contained in the text is what emerged out of their reflection on the issues of the day.

Life in captivity not only generated the need to remember and record the old stories but it also intensified a sense of belonging among the exiles. National allegiance to the temple no longer held the people together; rather, as they remembered their story through songs and poems, they recognised that this was now the bond that made them one.

In the exile, the collapse of the nation of Israel brought about an intense awareness of the unique character of Israel's relationship with God. Their enforced encounter with Babylonian culture and religion could have resulted in the complete collapse of their faith, but the people were determined not to allow this to happen, and they remained a worshipping community, united around what they recognised as God's law. But the exile also confronted them with a new view of the world. Being in Babylon at that time opened their eyes to wider cosmopolitan horizons: it was one of the most advanced civilisations of its time and a great superpower in the then-known world. The time had come for the exiles to look further than their own enclosed community, and, by doing so, they found that they could come to a deeper understanding of God's glory and majesty and his purpose in history. This enhanced understanding also gave them a new awareness of their role among the nations of the world. It is in this context that Isaiah's image of the 'servant' emerges (Isaiah 42; 49; 50; 52—53). The special role that the Jews were to play on the world scene was to be one of servanthood and of witness to the glory, power and faithfulness of their God. From now on, he was to be ever more accessible and close, not only to them but to other nations as yet outside the covenant relationship.

SIMPLY REMEMBERING WAS NOT ENOUGH

The turning point from despair to trust came as men such as Jeremiah, Ezekiel and Isaiah declared with utter confidence that God had accompanied the people on their difficult and involuntary pilgrimage to Babylon. The prophets drew on the rich imagery of testimony to God preserved from the past, but not simply for the sake of repeating it. They reinterpreted what they knew of God in the light of their experience in exile, heightening some elements, recasting past testimonies in new ways, and adding their own moving and heartfelt images of God's grace even in exile. They made use of every possible opportunity to remind the captive people that, through remembering their old stories, they would discover the resources needed to keep hope alive. The recurring but confident shout of the prophets was that, as in the past, God's promises of presence and care would prove trustworthy in the future (Isaiah 51:1–2). They were convinced that God's special covenant relationship with Israel had not been broken by the Babylonian conquest. Isaiah was one of the chief advocates of the crucial importance of memory. He summoned the people to remember their tradition and all that had happened to them long before the exile, and throughout his ministry he reminded them that God always kept his promises.

Memory alone would not have been enough on which to base all hopes, however. Memory as an end in itself becomes simply a preoccupation with the past. The prophets were convinced that 'remembering the story' had to be coupled with a hopeful anticipation of God's future (Isaiah 42:9–10; 43:19), but, crucially, that future was not going to be merely a repetition of the past. Even when the prophets used a familiar image or theme, it was often transformed in keeping with their trust that God was doing a 'new thing' (see, for example, Isaiah 51:9–10). Jeremiah spoke of the renewal of covenant, but it was not to be like the covenant of the past (Jeremiah 31:31–33). The image was now transformed because the experience of exile—of journeying into a distant and foreign land—had changed the nation dramatically.

EXILE AS METAPHOR

How, then, do we move from describing the historical events of the exile to using those events as a metaphor to begin discerning the signs of our own times? First we need to clarify what we mean by 'metaphor'. In essence, it means a situation, an image, a picture or something similar that is used symbolically in order to read and interpret some other situation better. At the same time, the original situation must remain unchanged and must be understood accurately, otherwise the metaphor will not be accurate.

We should not forget, either, that there can never be an exact relationship between the metaphor and the reality it is seeking to describe. It is the application of the metaphor—whether a story, image or character—that challenges us to see our own situation in new ways. The real power of a metaphor is the way in which it can bring two separate worlds into relationship through appropriate language. In the application of the metaphor, all sorts of connections can be made, but only if we are open to creativity and to the imagination—whether our own or those of the people around us. Such a task calls for careful explanation and wise understanding. This was the crucial pastoral role of the prophets as they accompanied the exiles—on the one hand, to be creative and imaginative, and, on the other hand, to offer helpful definitions and interpretation. There is a similar role for those who seek to guide and accompany Christian believers today.

EXILE AND PILGRIMAGE

It was as I led pilgrimages to various places and with diverse groups of people from all over the world that I first began using the idea of exile as a metaphor for understanding the current state of the church in the developed world. Through my theological studies I already knew about the significance of the Old Testament exile as a life-changing experience for those involved, and the leap from knowing that as a fact to using it with groups of people as a metaphor was not huge. I found that increasing numbers of people were being drawn to pilgrimage places either because they were at some kind of crossroads in their lives or because they were seeking a life-changing experience for themselves.

Most modern-day pilgrims I work with are already in some kind of relationship with the church—either fully committed and active, or lapsed and somewhat disillusioned. The use of exile as a metaphor with the former group helps them to see why the church is generally losing ground and finding itself on the margins of society. With the latter group, the metaphor has a much deeper impact and becomes immediately personal. It helps them to see their situation on the edge of the church in a different light, and to recognise that the insights arising from their 'exile experience' could be valuable not only to themselves but also to committed members of the church. I introduce the theme of exile at an early stage in a pilgrimage and we explore it in group reflections. It is usually when we compare the traditional institution of the church as it has become with the smaller groups of pilgrims that develop in the pilgrimage context—a very different kind of 'church'—that exile as a metaphor proves most useful. It is striking to hear pilgrims talk about how it helps them to understand their personal situation of exile in relation to the church or to interpret the church's relationship to the world as one of exile.

The relationship between exile and pilgrimage is therefore a crucial one. In one of his writings, C.S. Lewis makes an interesting distinction between what he calls 'pupil metaphors' and 'master metaphors' ('Bluspels and Flalansferes', in Max Black, *Importance of Language*, Prentice Hall, 1963). A pupil metaphor has an illustrative or teaching function, while the master metaphor is involved with a more fundamental perception of reality. In leading pilgrimages over the years, I have found Lewis's words to be true. Time and again I have used exile as a theme to encourage pilgrims to explore all sorts of faith and life issues. Subsequently, what happens is that exile becomes a 'pupil metaphor' that illuminates the practice of pilgrimage itself, and pilgrimage dominates as the 'master metaphor', illuminating the bigger concept of the 'journey of life'. It is this journey of life, this 'master metaphor', that is what people are fundamentally seeking to explore when they go on pilgrimage.

Part 2

Our captors asked for a song...
'Sing us one of the songs of Zion.'

PSALM 137:3

The exile in Babylon had been a huge faith-defining moment as well as a time of crisis out of which emerged an amazing process of theological reflection. As we look again at those days of exile, however, what becomes clear is that the crisis was essentially a quarrel not between the Jews and their captors but between the Jews and their God. When they arrived in Babylon, there was a strong sense that God had forgotten about them, so all they could think of doing was blaming him and adopting an attitude of despair. But the tradition of their faith—as they had understood it—could not cope with blame, despair and failure. Up until that point, the 'party line' had been quite straightforward: the God who had created them was the God who had led them out of captivity in Egypt and who continued to protect and nurture them. Now things had changed dramatically, and it was even possible that their understanding of the 'party line' itself felt a bit tired and worn out—certainly too tired and worn out to deal directly with this particular experience. Or could it be that their faith itself was on the verge of being forgotten because the years leading up to exile were characterised by complacency, religious laxity and different priorities?

Here is the key to understanding why the contemporary church has a great deal to learn from that Old Testament experience of exile. Despite the hardships of exile, the prophets knew it was essential to engage theologically with the big questions of life: where do we come from, where have we now come to and where are we hoping to arrive? The people themselves kept asking these same questions with a sense of urgency, in order to preserve their identity, protect their traditions and, above all, to preserve their story of God's creative and redeeming work. And these same questions make it theologically urgent for us today to engage realistically and faithfully with our own situation of exile.

REMEMBERING FOR THE FUTURE

The prophets of the Old Testament exile used what some modern scholars call 'faith memory' to ground the people in God's past and God's future, which would ultimately free them from the paralysis of the crisis of exile. As we saw in the previous chapter, the prophets drew the people gently but firmly to a place in their lives where they could enter into a process of sharing memory (see Isaiah 46:9; Deuteronomy 24:9; Nehemiah 1:8; Psalm 42:6). By remembering their story, they would rediscover those resources that would almost certainly rekindle the hope that God was present and active even in exile (Isaiah 54:7–8; Jeremiah 30:9; 33:14–26; Ezekiel 20:33–38).

The pastoral approach of the prophets in those days of crisis meant that memory and hope had to remain close together. They were quite certain that people's experience of God's renewal did not depend upon a transfiguration of what they had already experienced in the past—simply tweaking the system; rather, the renewal of their covenant with God would lead to a new experience of God being at work in their circumstances. The task of remembering gave the people a desperately needed sense of belonging and security, rooting them not only in a historic tradition but also in the experience of hoping for home. Without being mindful of their history, the exiles would have remained a restless and rootless people. The prophets were clear that by immersing themselves in mindfulness of God's creative and redeeming work, the people would discover lasting peace and joy—and this would be part of what would ultimately lead them 'home', both physically and figuratively.

In one of his published sermons (*Open to Judgement*, DLT, 1994), Rowan Williams argues strongly for the importance of what he calls 'remembering for the future' in our contemporary context. He suggests that memory is central in moving on, with hope and expectation, into the future. Salvation does not bypass history and memory; rather, it builds upon them and from them. Interestingly, in the Hebrew tradition the act of remembering does not mean looking back with nostalgia and attempting to recreate the past. Nor is it simply a collection of old names and dates or a clinging to past securities. It is, rather, an act of sharing the memory of how God has already created a relationship with his people and continues to work in and through them to fulfil his purposes. Throughout the Bible, any act of remembrance leads to a renewed sense of relationship with what has gone before (Isaiah 40:27–30; Psalm 107; Acts 2:14–36; Hebrews 1). This is the point of the Eucharist in the Christian tradition. It is not simply a recollection of something that happened 2000 years ago but an act of remembrance that leads to a renewed sense of the Christian's loving relationship with the Son of God and his self-sacrifice on the cross.

Memory and remembrance both remain central in any act of pilgrimage. My experience with pilgrims has shown me how essential it is that they leave behind two of the most potentially damaging ingredients in the contemporary understanding of re-membering—namely, regret and ambition. Harbouring regret prevents a person from moving on and ambition moves a person on too quickly from the opportunities of the present moment. Pilgrims have to take on board a different way of remembering, one that is rooted firmly both in history and in hope. So often, on pilgrimage, participants realise they need time and space to understand their own past and to seek the healing of some memories. Indeed, one of the most important principles of pilgrimage is that before we can embrace any kind of new life or new start—which pilgrims often seek—there needs to be a recovering and reconciling of our past stories. Sorting out our relationship with the past equips us to embrace the future in a much more authentic way, because what is not remembered cannot be healed. For pilgrims, as for those long-ago Babylonian exiles, the present is very much in the future and the future is connected to the present, but it's the recovery and healing of the past that enables them to journey together in hope towards a sense of radical freedom in God, which is our ultimate home. We remember and are healed and are then set free to face the future with hope, instead of despair that we will never truly come home.

HEIRS OF THE STORY

Journeying together to places of pilgrimage is not simply a history lesson with a bit of worship thrown in for good measure. It is a most effective opportunity for Christians not only to remember their personal story but also to discover ways to maintain and strengthen their faith, and the faith of one another, in order to face the ongoing realities of life. The rituals of pilgrimage give people the chance to re-evaluate these realities and discover ways to abandon unhelpful patterns of behaviour and erroneous views about God and faith, which disrupt the authentic and balanced living that is God's intention for his people.

My hunch is that, in their pastoral ministry to the distressed exiles, the Old Testament prophets not only reminded them of their story but convinced them that they were actually part of that story as it continued to unfold. Similarly, pilgrims today don't merely commemorate a sacred place by visiting it; they actually embody that place—especially if they go there regularly, as is often the case. This is the difference between a pilgrim and a tourist: tourists pass through a particular place but, for pilgrims, that place, as it were, passes through them. Visiting Durham Cathedral, a tourist will take photos, tour the sights and tick it off the mental 'to do' list, whereas a pilgrim will pause to ponder St Cuthbert's evangelistic ministry in the seventh century and the way in which the Lindisfarne Gospels, produced by his community, continue to inspire people today. In this way, by remembering, pilgrims not only identify a sacred space but identify themselves as the heirs of that place's story and find renewal there. As he spoke through the prophets to the people of the exile, so God continues to speak to the pilgrim, showing the way towards a new way of relating and being, one that is created over and over and over again by his grace—a way that is profoundly different from our world of profit, power and status. In the final part of this book, I will return to this theme to show how such renewal can happen in practice and in particular places.

In the next two chapters I want to do three things. First I want to define what I mean by today's 'situation of exile'; then I want to show how and why we are in an exile situation; and finally I want to suggest ways out of exile, or how to find our way home.

＊

———— *Chapter 3* ————

EXPERIENCING EXILE AGAIN

Exile is defined and explained in many ways by many people. A popular modern dictionary definition explains it in personal terms—that exiles are banished people compelled by circumstances to reside away from their native land. Patrick Whitworth, in a book on spirituality and mission for a 'church in exile' (*Prepare for Exile*, SPCK, 2008), lists a number of ways in which people find themselves in exile situations. They could have lost the familiar environment that gives them identity and meaning—ranging from youngsters leaving home for the first time to those who are refugees or victims of divorce. In psychological terms they could be people who have, for whatever reason, lost their security and well-being, perhaps as a hospital patient without independence or control, or through experiencing some kind of acute bereavement or loss. As we have already seen, there is also the metaphorical meaning— becoming a stranger in a strange land with a significant sense of loss of home, indeed of any sense of a place of belonging.

EXILE TODAY

In Chapter 1, I mentioned the huge contribution that Walter Brueggemann has made both to Old Testament scholarship generally and to the study of the exile in particular. His scholarship is unusual in the sense that he is eager to catch any possible opportunity to link the historic with the contemporary, the past with the present. In historical terms, he shows how the Babylonian exiles experienced the loss of a reliable and structured world that gave meaning and coherence to their lives. In pastoral terms, he argues that many people have a similar sense of exile today, feeling abandoned and questioning the moral coherence of life, while at the same time being preoccupied with their own situation. To put it bluntly, they are asking repeatedly, 'For heaven's sake, where do I find meaning?'

In his book *Dwelling in a Strange Land* (Canterbury Press, 2003), biblical scholar John Holdsworth picks up Brueggemann's pastoral response to the current situation of exile but argues that rather than being in exile, the church itself has become a refuge for exiles. Accordingly, we need to construct a fresh pastoral theology to enable an adequate response to these circumstances. To bring this about, there needs to be a wide and genuine conversation between all sorts of people and agencies both within and outside the church. It is my belief that pilgrimage can provide an appropriate place for such a conversation, as the act of pilgrimage is itself a spiritual laboratory in which Christians can start to work out what it means to be a church today, whether in exile or for exiles.

The bottom line of the Old Testament exile was that there were two very distinct groups of people involved. As we have already seen, one group was made up of captives taken to Babylon, held there against their will as a marginalised and humiliated minority. The other group was left behind in Jerusalem and became an impoverished and broken assortment of people, sitting around a ruined temple and reminiscing about the good old days. The task facing both groups was daunting. The group in Babylon had to set in motion a process of major acclimatisation in order to reassess many of their cherished traditions and beliefs, given their new context. Those gathered in what was left of the temple precincts had to come to terms not only with the destruction of their sacred place but also with how to live within a stone's throw of the ruins, before they could start clearing the rubble and find a new way forward. The tasks facing both groups must have been mentally and physically exhausting, and not remotely glamorous. They had lost three of the most important comfort blankets of the good old days—profit, power and status—but at least they now had the chance to start establishing some new foundations.

Our current situation of exile is reminiscent of the experiences of both these ancient groups of people. In many parts of the developed world, and certainly in Europe, there are Christians and churches who have become completely marginalised from positions of influence, responsibility and power. Sadly, they persist in functioning as if all is well. They continue to offer answers to questions that people stopped asking more than a generation ago, and behave as if the noises they make actually still matter. Then there are other churches who cannot deny the exile context, because they are sitting around in ruins, telling each other tales about the good old times. Tragically, far too many people have long since walked away from the church altogether, abandoning what they feel to be a sinking Titanic, only glancing back to ask mockingly, 'Sing us one of the songs of Zion' (Psalm 137:3). The churches continue to sing in their own way but hardly anyone listens—and when some actually bother to do so, too many have forgotten what the 'song' means, so they walk away once again. This is our current exile.

ASPECTS OF EXILE AND SIGNS OF HOPE

Just as in the Old Testament exile, the exile situation we face today involves a combination of both religious and non-religious aspects. In Babylon it was impossible to disentangle the religious concerns of the day from the politics, and our own situation of exile is in some ways similar. We now need to take a brief look at the signs of exile as they appear both in our church and in our society, so as to add background to what I will go on to say about the importance of pilgrimage in the wider scheme of things.

One of the most thought-provoking commentaries that I have read on the issues that concern many people today is Carol Ann Duffy's 'Ode to Christmas', a stinging critique of much that she feels is wrong in the world today. The poem updates the traditional 'Twelve days of Christmas' to highlight issues such as the plight of the families of soldiers fighting in Afghanistan and all those whose lives are devastated by floods and famine. She also fires verbal bullets at MPs over their expenses and at the bankers over their profits, and ends with a comment on global climate change.

For me, the key passage is the one that deals with the fifth day of Christmas, where Duffy offers her own version of the five gold rings:

The first gold ring was gold indeed—
bankers' profits fired in greed.

The second ring outshone the sun,
fuelled by carbon, doused by none.

Ring three was black gold, O for oil—
a serpent swallowing its tail.

The fourth ring was Celebrity;
Fool's Gold, winking on TV.

Ring five, religion's halo, slipped—
a blind for eyes or gag for lips.

With these five gold rings they you wed,
then slip them off when you are dead.

As I lead pilgrimages, I find that the main concerns of those journeying together, trying to make some sense of the world and seeking ways to move out of a situation of exile, are a combination of similar issues. The greed embodied in the financial markets, global warming and the stark inequalities in the political response, the huge influence of oil production on political decision-making and the madness of celebrity culture are all issues that I have heard pilgrims bemoan and pray about. And there is so much more—the violence in our cities, gang warfare, escalation of drug abuse, the ever-growing inequality between rich and poor, the rampant spread of AIDS, the bloody clashes between religious groups in many countries and the spread of international terrorism. In the face of these concerns, there is a crisis of hope throughout the developed world, a crisis leading to a serious collective depression, which is another manifestation of our exile.

What about exile in terms of the church? Because the church is deeply and intimately connected with the kingdom of God as it continues to reveal itself in the here and now, the task of identifying signs of an exile mindset in the life of our church communities is imperative. In an unpublished sermon, it was a retired Anglican priest living in Wales, Michael Walls, who not only introduced me to Carol Ann Duffy's 'Ode to Christmas', but reworked her Fifth Day of Christmas lines to highlight some of the issues relevant to the church's situation of exile:

First gold ring is men still to the fore,
when willing women wait at the door.

Second ring is putting unreal unity first
before true unity in love and service.

Third ring is rules that keep us away
when welcome to all should rule the day.

Ring four is resistance to scholarly finds
when revealing ideas light up minds.

Fifth is reluctance to speak loud and clear
of Truth we believe but also fear.

I find that many modern pilgrims are preoccupied with a combination of these same issues, which they feel are pushing them to the margins of the church. Women in far too many parts of the church continue to be treated unequally, while commitment to church unity is based at best on empty dreams and at worst on hypocrisy. Rules owing more to human prejudice than biblical truth continue to shout at some people that they are unacceptable and whisper to others that they are OK. At the same time, there are too many within the church who are either afraid or unable to stand up against these and other injustices and misinterpretations of our faith story.

Fortunately, there are clear signs of hope in many different parts of the church in many different places. There are people who remember what the old 'songs' really meant, and they have already begun to put in place new ways to retell the story. Like those who found themselves in Babylon, so there are people today who recognise that the call to prophetic proclamation is far more urgent and important than simply choosing to make do with worn-out memories. Like their biblical predecessors, these contemporary prophetic voices are doing their best to make sense of living in what has become, metaphorically, a strange and foreign land.

Similarly, like those who stayed behind in Jerusalem, many are opting to engage theologically and practically with changed times, and are working to relate to the old sacred and often ruined places in a new way. There are those who are bold and strong enough to begin the difficult task of clearing the rubble and looking forward in hope, despite the detractors who are sitting around and watching them. Just as for the people of the long-ago exile, the task facing us today is exhausting and unglamorous, but nevertheless urgent. Like them, we have lost the old comfort blankets of the good old days—profit, power and status—but, even so, we have the chance to give it another go and start laying new foundations.

PILGRIM SEEKERS

As I mentioned earlier, on the whole, pilgrims are those who already have a connection with the church. Many of them are regular faithful worshippers in one of the many Christian denominations and come on pilgrimage either as part of their own church's programme or as participants in a pilgrimage that they have seen advertised. Others are not such regular worshippers and may have consciously chosen to distance themselves from the church, because of disillusionment or anger or despair at what they see happening within it. Despite their distancing, however, most of them claim that they continue to remain faithful to God and worship and nurture their faith in alternative ways. It is interesting that not many pilgrims would regard themselves as 'lapsed Christians'; they would be reasonably well versed in church matters, spirituality and the scriptures. In my experience, pilgrimages almost always include people from both of these two groups, brought together not necessarily by design but by a common desire to visit and explore the history and spirituality of a particular place.

The time and energy I spend with these diverse groups are precious because pilgrims tend to be people who are open to discussion. The sharing of experiences comes naturally to them and, as they pause at different places, this shared exploration of past stories, along with their vision and hopes for the future, is drawn out by the present moment. Holy space has an amazing knack of doing that! These experiences with pilgrims constantly bring home to me, first, the fact that we are most certainly in a situation of exile today and, second, what that exile is all about—the dislocation of church and culture and of faith and life. It is worth remembering that exile never pushes people to become pilgrims; it's always the other way around. Pilgrims are those who, through a shared experience of journey, come to recognise the signs of exile in themselves, in the church and in society, and choose to become active in the task of seeking ways home and singing the old songs differently. I once led an ecumenical pilgrimage to Santiago de Compostela. The pilgrims were a mixed group of Anglicans, Catholics and Presbyterians and, although the group gelled well from the beginning, there was tension when the Eucharist was celebrated. As a group of faithful Christians who worshipped regularly, they had always been aware of the rules regarding the receiving of Holy Communion. But journeying together drew out the acuteness of the sense of 'them and us', of who can and who can't receive. What had once been 'paper rules' now affected the whole of this gathered group and became a situation of exile. However, the actual experience of pilgrimage to a holy place made the group even more determined to seek different ways to 'sing the old songs' and to strive for unity in new ways.

THIRSTING FOR HOPE

In a piece of masterly theological reflection (*The Moral Sense*, James Wilson and Jonathan Sacks, The Smith Institute, 2002), the Chief Rabbi Jonathan Sacks asks us to imagine what it would be like to take a nephew or niece for a ride on the London Eye. As the wheel turns, the great buildings of Whitehall and Westminster come into view and the youngster asks, 'What do they do there?' We answer that this is the seat of government, and the people in those buildings produce and distribute law and power. As we get to the top of the wheel, the Stock Exchange, surrounded by shops and offices, comes into view and the youngster asks again, 'What do they do there?' This time we answer that it is the home of the financial markets, and the people in those buildings produce and distribute money and wealth. Then we see St Paul's Cathedral and the smaller towers and spires of neighbouring churches, and the youngster asks for the third time, 'What do they do there?' The answer to this question is more difficult. The most natural thing to say is that these are houses of worship—but if we did say that, our nephew or niece would probably notice a change in our response and would almost certainly go on to ask, 'Well, what do they produce and distribute there?' It would be tempting this time to say to the youngster, 'But those buildings are not that kind of place.' Jonathan Sacks points out that if we answered in that way, we would be committing one of the most defining errors of our culture—the error of forgetting what faith actually does produce and distribute. At the heart of our exile today is our ignorance of what this 'something' is and our inability to answer accurately the youngster's question.

Being on pilgrim journeys with people has convinced me that, despite the current sense of exile, this is an exciting faith moment in the life of the church. So, to the nephew or niece's question about the houses of worship—'What do they produce and distribute there, Uncle?'—I would want to answer, 'Ways of living and sharing the Christian story of hope.'

'But why, Uncle?'

'Well, because the world is thirsting for it, my dear.'

Today's exile is about this thirst, and the Christian story of hope is about the knowledge that good will ultimately and always triumph over evil, that the kingdom of God will come, and that one day all death and suffering will cease to be. Hope, as a defining human quality, has a profound impact on the way people choose to live and choose to prioritise, but hope can never be a road map. Although it is essential to know the promised ending of the story of our faith, it can only be the 'old songs', the story as it has already unfolded, that we can know absolutely for certain.

Historically, we have seen how the perpetrators of the Soviet gulag, the concentration camps and gas chambers of World War II, the killing fields in Cambodia, the genocide in Rwanda and the 9/11 bombings all believed that they possessed accurate road maps leading towards an ideal future. But their hopes ended in destruction, and their planning and mapping and hoping led to the brutal deaths of millions. It is probable that they didn't set out to be 'evil' but to follow their beliefs to the bitter end—and evil was an inevitable result.

One of the paradoxes of the events remembered on Maundy Thursday is that, at the start of the last supper, the gathered disciples must have been pretty certain that they too possessed a road map and that the future was clear. The miracles that they had witnessed with Jesus must have convinced them that glory lay ahead, rather than the way of the cross. As supper ended, however, they were shocked to learn that this was not the case. Instead, they were left with no real story to tell. After eating the bread and drinking the wine, their expectations for the future disappeared; the 'old songs' were lost, as it were, because as Jesus' after-dinner speech continued (John 14—17), the disciples recognised that events would unfold very differently from how they had expected. Timothy Radcliffe makes clear the challenge of what happened when Judas sold Jesus and Peter denied him, while the others disappeared quietly (*Why Go to Church?* Continuum, 2008). At that very moment, he says, the community that had surrounded Jesus and supported his public ministry disintegrated, and the founding story of the Christian Church became the collapse of any story that predicts an easy path to glory.

When we remember the story as it has already unfolded, we learn that by placing our hope in the ultimate coming of God's kingdom, we are not provided with a road map that we can simply follow into the future; we are provided with faith. Paradoxically, our relationship with God deepens and becomes more intimate when we stop deluding ourselves that we know what the future holds: it is only the one who holds the future that we can possibly know for certain. The current exile should not fill us with despair and fear, because we need to remember that the Church itself was born in a crisis of exile. Out of the crisis of exile, authentic and honest hope will always emerge.

HOPE AND THE CREATIVITY OF GOD

By authentic and honest hope, I mean a confidence that the infinite creativity of God will bring good out of evil and communion out of the crisis of exile. This hope is not a hope that simply points to the future; rather, it is one that enables and allows the future to break into the present moment. As Christians, we hope for the coming of the kingdom of God, knowing that we already have one foot in that kingdom. As that future kingdom broke into the world in the life of Jesus, so the same kingdom continues to break into the world whenever people share God's life and whenever people succeed in overcoming hatred with love. Timothy Radcliffe sums this up well when he says that this is the kind of hope that means 'daring to find God's eternity glancing through the clouds now'. He encourages fellow pilgrims to dream with him that what will emerge from the present situation of exile will be humbler, simpler, less optimistic but far more deeply rooted in authentic and honest hope.

It is this hope that those houses of worship, seen from the London Eye, produce and distribute. But if we are part of the production and distribution team, there is still much work for us to do. We will need to produce powerful signs that will enable others to catch a glimpse of the hopeful future that lies ahead and encourage them to share in the task of enabling still others to glimpse it. And, as we will consider further, the act of pilgrimage is a vital resource in this most important of tasks.

❖

—————— *Chapter 4* ——————

PROPHETIC OR PATHETIC?

The effectiveness of the Old Testament prophetic ministry lay in its awakening of the people's memory of its past so as to recover a spirit to cope with their crisis. To ensure that our response to today's crisis of faith remains prophetic, hope must be found precisely where hope seems lost. In order to transcend so much that is shortsighted in modern-day living, prophetic communities will need to imagine new countercultural ways of coping with our situation of exile, ways that recall to mind the 'old songs' and the story of God's faithfulness to his children through human history. There is a serious need for us all to hear and heed the prophetic voices of today, otherwise our circumstances will almost certainly remain no more than pathetic.

KEEPING HOPE AT THE HEART OF OUR REFLECTION

The truth of the matter is that it's not just isolated 'signs of hope' that we are called to seek but a more serious consideration of hope itself as a pillar of our faith and the very backbone of all that stands against exile. One of the most important modern-day Christian theologians of hope is Jürgen Moltmann, and in one of his writings (*The Experiment Hope*, SCM, 1975) he provocatively quotes the Marxist humanist writer Ernst Bloch: 'Where there is hope, there is religion; where there is religion, there is not always hope.' A great deal of Moltmann's work is devoted to the central idea that hope has a vital role to play in Christian theological engagement. Indeed, in most of the world's religions, people's hopes are safe-guarded not only by personal faith but by the framework of the religious tradition itself. By the same token, however, Moltmann challenges those religious traditions to recognise that, all too often, hope is abolished, betrayed and rendered ineffective by their mismanagement of what has been entrusted to them. At the heart of Moltmann's thinking, hope as a spiritual experience remains crucial to our understanding of the search for the ultimate meaning of life. This is the authentic hope that does not deceive or limit people—or simply shout at them—but opens up new horizons and fresh paths out of exile.

Christian teaching on hope does stress, however, that it's not simply about having a number of isolated hopes at our disposal. It means, rather, hope in the sense of being completely open to the realities that lie ahead. Conversely, despair, as the opposite of hope, does not mean burying a few hopes here or destroying a few illusions there; it means giving up our openness to future possibilities and moving to a position of being fundamentally closed. To hope means to be in a state of preparedness, neither tying ourselves to what has passed by nor losing ourselves to wishing and dreaming. We should not think of hope as something that one person has and another doesn't. It is, rather, a primal mode of existing; all being well, people hope as long as they live and live as long as they hope.

The hopeful person is always an explorer and a discoverer who looks over one shoulder at what has been but also ahead to what might be. In hope, we recognise every situation in which we find ourselves as a station on the journey that we must travel in order to realise who and what we are as human beings. Only then can we grasp that hope is much more than feeling cheerful. It is the belief that, as God's children, we are on our way into the future with a confidence that our life can and must have ultimate meaning. This confidence means we can trust that we will find ways out of the current situation of exile, no matter how bleak things may seem at times.

THE PROPHETIC TASK

In his correspondence with the Benedictine scholar Jean Leclercq, Thomas Merton identified prophecy and not survival as one of the most urgent tasks facing the church in the modern world (*Survival or Prophecy?*, ed. Patrick Hart, Farrar Strauss Giroux, 2002). It was the prophets that offered pastoral care and support to the exiles of the sixth century and it was the prophetic voice that sustained them as they emerged out of exile. Today the prophetic function remains basically twofold. First, the prophet is called to speak directly to a given situation and to insist that, despite appearances, God is in the present moment, in power and also in judgment. Second, the prophet must interpret that situation and disclose that, despite appearances, God will work through the present moment to bring about his invincible ends.

The Catholic theologian Hans Küng bemoans the fact (*Judaism*, SCM, 1992) that this voice of prophecy was more or less silenced after the Old Testament exile had ended and that, on the people's return to Jerusalem, there was no real counterbalance to the institution of the temple. There was no prophetic protest against the legalism, ritualism and clericalism that developed in the aftermath of exile, a protest proclaiming the sovereign freedom of God himself as opposed to the political freedom of the people. Clearly the office of prophet was generally diluted in this period, with some continuing merely as scribes rather than as much-needed charismatic prophets (Psalm 74:9). It is clear that the more the prophetic influence declined, the stronger religious legalism became. How things have not changed!

The quenching of prophecy even in our own day is a further

mark of our current exile. Hans Küng poses three sobering questions in the light of this loss. First, are we doing sufficient justice to the prophetic task of being the conscience of society? Contemporary prophecy should call for an abolition of social injustice, an end to the gulf between rich and poor, between the privileged and the underprivileged. The Church, he says, surely has a ministry of social criticism. Second, are we doing sufficient justice to the prophetic task of admonishing ethical irresponsibility? Contemporary prophecy should call for the well-being of all people and condemn war as a political means towards lasting peace. The Church, he says, surely has a ministry of political criticism. Third, are we doing sufficient justice to the prophetic task of trusting in the power of God's word? Contemporary prophecy should call for a deep criticism of pagan ideologies—false gods, autocratic powers and rulers who dress up their personal agendas in the name of religion. The Church, Küng says, surely has a ministry of theological criticism.

In several places, Walter Brueggemann suggests that in the face of what he calls 'the death systems of the world' (and what we have been calling 'exile'), the contemporary prophetic voice has been entrusted with the task of offering an alternative to a world that has failed in its extravagant claims and lacks any life-giving power. We see the supreme example of such an alternative in the events of the final days of Holy Week. In the Gospels, three days stand out: Friday, Saturday and Sunday. In the events surrounding the end of Jesus' life, Friday symbolised the exposure of a vulnerable God in the face of an empire's violence. Brueggemann is certain that, on that Friday, Jesus' trial before Pilate turned out to be the trial of an empire before Jesus, and that his conviction and death paradoxically emerged as the most supreme display of power and authority that the world has ever seen. On that Friday, the world was exposed as utterly fraudulent in its claim to offer an authentic meaning to life. It can only ever be a place of exile. Saturday was a day of fear, regret and silence, but by Sunday there was a tremendous, world-shaking turn of events. Those events were the epitome of surprise and hope, behind which lay the wonder of comprehensive restoration and an authentic homecoming from exile.

In some ways, those three days take us right back to the Babylonian exile. On Friday, the people are faced with destruction and dislocation. On Saturday, they are mocked for their faith and scorned for its failure, forced to 'sing the songs of Zion' in a very strange land. On Sunday, however, exile ends and the people are restored—this time neither to a holy city nor to a place built by human hands, but to the core of life itself. In the resurrection, true meaning is restored to everything and everyone, and the entire creation bears witness to our creative and redeeming God.

At the heart of the contemporary prophetic task, then, lies an invitation to journey as pilgrims together, from the vulnerability of Friday through the dark silence of Saturday and into the surprise and joy of Sunday, where 'coming home' from exile means discovering God as a precious gift, himself offering lasting freedom and hope. It is an awesome task, peppered with dangers and obstacles—a major one being that of denial. In the Old Testament exile, many Jews were content to deny that the calamity of defeat by Babylon could ever happen (Jeremiah 6:13–15; 8:10–12; 28:1–17; Ezekiel 13). In today's situation of exile, denial and pretence remain dominant attitudes. Even when calamity strikes, now as then, there are those who resist moving away from a situation of despair and insist, instead, on remaining in the ruined precincts of what once was.

BUILDING PROPHETIC COMMUNITIES

My hunch is that a lone and lonely prophetic voice today will not be heard. Instead, the prophetic voice will be best heard when spoken by communities. The contemporary moral philosopher Alasdair MacIntyre makes an interesting observation in respect of such prophetic communities (*After Virtue*, Duckworth, 1993).

He envisages the history of humanity as written in three stages. The first stage was a time of great flourishing, a time when people understood each other and lived in harmony together. The second stage was one of catastrophe and revolution, when people grew tired of harmony and threw a whole variety of life experiences and choices into a melting pot, thinking that they knew best. The third stage was one of regret and exile, when the people wished they had not played God. They returned to the melting pot only to find that the fire had almost destroyed everything. All they could salvage were fragments of the old ideas and patterns of life. As they picked out these fragments, they were unable to put them back together properly and the old stuff of life remained disjointed and unrelated. But MacIntyre's main point is that this task of joining up the bits can never be done by individuals alone. Real and lasting hope lies in the construction of local forms of prophetic community where the mending can be done together.

Faith has a crucial role to play in the construction of such prophetic communities, which can offer a way out of exile. Both within the church and in the global non-religious context, the mindset of exile will always be tempted to pursue profit, power and status—the familiar comfort blankets. Constructing life patterns around profit, power and status will never generate the common good, however; nor will it provide a viable route to the kingdom of God.

DOING IT LIKE JESUS

In recognising the importance of constructing such local prophetic communities, we are nevertheless not given permission to ignore the challenges of globalisation. We cannot ignore the fact that over 80 per cent of the world's population is desperately poor; nor can we overlook the destructive effect that this poverty has on what it means to be human. In commending a locally rooted prophetic perspective as a way to authentic and hope-filled living, we cannot allow such a perspective to be parochial, concerned only with the immediate context. At the same time, given our culture's assumption that we achieve our aspirations by the accumulation of profit, power and status, I would argue that the local level is where we have most scope to embody a prophetic perspective that will draw on alternative values and begin to create a genuine counterculture.

In *Transforming Mission* (Orbis, 1992), his influential contribution to the theology of mission, David Bosch observes the importance of three things. First, the kind of mission that encompasses the whole of life calls for close interplay between working for the kingdom of God by social action and witnessing to the salvation that Jesus brings. Second, in the developed world we have allowed 'salvation' to be dominant, so that we read the Gospels as if they were only long introductions to the death and resurrection of Jesus. Third, holistic mission calls for equal attention to the whole life of Jesus, not only the end of it. Indeed, a faith that transforms a people in exile as well as the structures and processes of society has to take the importance of the whole life of Jesus far more seriously. I have already mentioned that the last Friday, Saturday and Sunday of the earthly life of Jesus are at the core of the Christian faith. We need to remember, though, that the central claim of those three days—the crucifixion, burial and resurrection of Jesus; his vulnerability, silence and surprise—is firmly linked to his whole life from Bethlehem to Calvary. The last three days are the endpoint of Jesus' entire earthly ministry and the experiences of all those who met him and were transformed by that encounter.

Ann Morisy's work as a contemporary community theologian and writer picks up the prophetic idea of taking on board the whole life of Jesus as foundational to the journey home from exile. In a clergy training day for the Diocese of Bangor (2008), she highlighted a number of distinctives in the life of Jesus that are key issues for this metaphorical journey home. First, throughout his ministry Jesus tends to avoid power, yet also shows an amazing ability to use power in a righteous way, thus showing an important difference between being powerful and being authoritative. He seems to make a point of resisting whatever might lead to his becoming powerful in worldly terms: his entry into Jerusalem on a donkey is an example. Another important distinctive is the way in which he is willing to risk being overwhelmed, rather than constantly working to be in control all the time: his overturning of the money changers' tables in the temple, for example, could well have landed him in prison there and then. He is also willing to take risks with rules and regulations in a way that might anger the religious establishment. He subverts the status quo and challenges the assumed ways of doing and understanding things, especially in relation to religious practice.

Jesus is always keen for his concern for others to go well beyond family, neighbour and tribal circles. This can be seen at the wedding in Cana and in his words to the apostle John from the cross, when he gives his mother into his friend's care. He avoids tit-for-tat behaviour by stepping back from escalating differences, but he is also unafraid to stand his ground. He invests in the most unlikely of people: those whom Jesus chooses are not the most obvious 'top team'. In fact, very often they have already been written off by others. At all times, Jesus avoids the 'them and us' syndrome and the splitting of people into categories of 'clean' and 'unclean'; he resists saying that some are 'in' and others 'out'. By actively embracing those who are different or rejected by the mainstream, he completely transforms ways of operating both in terms of faith and in terms of society. Finally, he communicates by simple story and clear analogy rather than by rational, moralistic and sociological analysis.

Ann Morisy argues that Christian spiritual formation involves regularly rehearsing or practising the prophetic approach that Jesus demonstrated in his life and ministry. 'Doing it like Jesus', far from being a pious platitude, is in fact a powerful and countercultural way of standing against the dominating values of profit, power and status. As we start to embrace such a prophetic approach, so we will start to experience the wonderful and liberating generosity that is symptomatic of the grace of God. Grace does not have winners or losers: each one of us falls short of the winning line. God's generosity is such, however, that we only have to move towards the way in which Jesus lived his life for a cascade of God's grace to be triggered. We are not called to do everything as Jesus would have done—we can't. Grace comes flowing whenever we offer an alternative prophetic approach, regardless of how modest it is.

At the heart of our local prophetic communities, a new vision for our times will emerge, which is at the same time a retelling of our faith story, a new way of singing the 'old songs'. This vision encompasses the rebuilding of the church in the midst of our restless and fragmentary society, which has lost a clear sense of where it belongs, from where it has come and to where it is journeying. It is my firm belief that the experience of pilgrimage today can offer a way for this prophetic work to start to happen. Is it a coincidence that, while so many churches are emptying, more and more people are flocking to places of pilgrimage, searching for meaning and for authentic hope? I think not, and I want to turn next to the reasons why this is the case.

Part 3

How shall we sing the Lord's song in a strange land?

PSALM 137:4

Having considered what we mean by 'exile', and also having reflected on our current state of exile both in church and in society, we will now focus in detail on how the experience of pilgrimage can help to lead the church from a sense of exile and towards a sense of homecoming. In spite of our state of exile, the paradox is that in many ways this is an exciting time for the church, and in Parts 3 and 4 of this book we will consider why this is the case. Pilgrimage is a timely challenge to the contemporary church. The hundreds of thousands of people who gather at the world's pilgrimage sites can teach our somewhat tired and burnt-out faith communities some vital lessons about their current situation and the opportunities available for connection and transformation.

As I stated earlier, pilgrimage is a universal religious phenomenon. Each year, millions of people make pilgrimages. Buddhists and Baha'is, Hindus, Muslims, Jews, Christians and Sikhs all travel to shrines and holy places. In much of their religious practice, these people may appear to have little in common, but they all share the desire to go on pilgrimage, a journey that is in part a search for meaning as well as for spiritual advancement. It is a journey that reflects the recovery of a sense of the sacredness of place and landscape in a fragile world and the widespread desire to connect with roots and traditions. Indeed, a place of pilgrimage is generally regarded as a place of intersection between everyday life and the life of God. It is a geographical location that is worthy of reverence because it has been the scene of a manifestation of divine power or has an association with a holy person. Such ideas are common to almost every world religion, yet what fundamentally distinguishes a Christian pilgrimage from any other is the Christian's search for Christ. Even when the destination is the tomb of a saint, this quest for Christ is never lost, because the saints are important only as so many examples of different ways to imitate Christ.

The practice of pilgrimage is one way in which the church can respond to a deep-seated desire in people both to travel and to have a few fixed points in their mobile lives. Places of pilgrimage can be special places of meeting, places where the spiritual and the material come together, and places where people might have a sense of home more significant than the neighbourhood of their present home. In the pilgrimage experience, both the journey and the arrival become parts of the one activity and both can be a means to spiritual growth. David Osborne, a member of the Iona Community, refers to it as a means of tapping into something that is deep in the human unconscious (*Pilgrimage*, Grove, 1996).

My personal commitment to pilgrimage has been influenced by the place in which I live and work, the Llyn Peninsula in north-west Wales. It's an area not only of outstanding physical beauty but also where the Christian tradition has been vibrant for over 1500 years. The increasing pilgrimage traffic that I have observed in recent years demonstrates the urge of Christians today to rediscover the historical importance and significance of pilgrimage, both as a leisure pastime and also as another way of worshipping and learning with other Christians. The opportunity of sharing in other people's pilgrimages, as a participant and as a leader for both groups and individuals, has shown me the importance of the whole experience and that pilgrimage can be a vital source of renewal and inspiration for today's church. It is interesting that so many of the world's pilgrimage sites are places of immense antiquity. It is precisely in the rediscovery of the church's distant past, particularly of those times when the faith community was most vibrant and challenging, that Christians find new vision not only for the contemporary church but for the future.

✳

———— *Chapter 5* ————

WHY GO ON PILGRIMAGE? RELIGION AND SACRED PLACE

Christians can justifiably regard themselves as the pilgrim people of God. Indeed, in the Bible, the idea of the spiritual life as a journey is expressed often. For instance, the exodus was a spiritual experience in the sense that it was a direct response by a group of people to God's invitation to journey. The 40-year period was a time when the people's faith was tested, their obedience checked and their relationship with God strengthened. Through the centuries, pilgrims have journeyed to sacred places to seek healing, inspiration and redirection, or to mark a significant moment in their lives. Often it has been a quest by simple, practical and down-to-earth people to find 'stepping stones' between themselves and the geographically distant and spiritually abstract concepts of the Christian faith. The theologian and pilgrimage leader Ian Bradley, in his recent book *Pilgrimage: A Cultural and Spiritual Journey* (Lion, 2009), says that many people find it easier to walk than to talk their faith and that they derive encouragement through walking in the footsteps of countless pilgrims before them. In that sense, 'pilgrimage' as a means to becoming church in a different way is not a new phenomenon. It is actually as old as the church itself and, as a Christian practice, it has probably always challenged the religious establishment in some ways. This challenge has often focused on the ambivalent relationship between the inner, spiritual journey of faith and the outward, everyday journey of life, because pilgrimage always involves an individual encountering God directly rather than through the hierarchy and systems of the church.

Peter Millar states that an outward pilgrimage is often a powerful sign of an inner journey—of repentance, resurrection and rebirth —a journey of the heart, which is held in the Creator's hands (*An Iona Prayer Book*, Canterbury Press, 1998). It is rooted in the conviction that the life of faith is a process of continual change and movement. Christians are never static; they carry within themselves a sense of expectancy, of looking forward in hope. The writer of the letter to the Hebrews framed this hope in memorable words: 'Therefore, since we are surrounded by so great a cloud of witnesses, let us also lay aside every weight and the sin that clings so closely, and let us run with perseverance the race that is set before us, looking to Jesus the pioneer and perfecter of our faith' (Hebrews 12:1–2, NRSV). Here is expressed the journey of the Christian on a continuing pilgrimage towards God—a pilgrimage that will never be completed here on earth but continues in God's eternal kingdom.

ASKING THE BIG QUESTIONS

As I wrote in my introduction to *Every Pilgrim's Guide to Celtic Britain and Ireland*, in his book *Footprints of the Northern Saints* (DLT, 1996), the former Archbishop of Westminster Basil Hume raised some serious questions that many people find themselves asking: 'What is life all about? What are we here for? Where is it all leading to? What happens after death?' According to Hume, the early northern Celtic saints brought answers to these questions, and those answers are as relevant today as they were in the sixth and seventh centuries. The act of pilgrimage still echoes questions that emerge for each of us from time to time. What is the reason for my being? What does it mean for me to seek God? It is surely no coincidence that many who go on pilgrimage are at transitional stages of life, people who are having to make some big life decisions, people who are trying to cope with life-changing circumstances.

It is true that, throughout history, some have regarded pilgrimage as a kind of 'escape from reality', a means of avoiding constraints and tensions. Similarly, groups of pilgrims today will include participants with all sorts of strange and wonderful reasons for coming along. However, many people who begin their pilgrimages for reasons that have little to do with faith speak retrospectively about their surprise that the journey touched places of personal interior pain, uncertainty and vulnerability as well as joy.

As I again mentioned in my earlier guide book to Celtic pilgrimage sites, another pilgrimage leader, Cintra Pemberton, remarks on how the line between being a 'pilgrim' and being a 'tourist' can sometimes be very fluid (*Soulfaring*, SPCK, 1999). The starting point—whether simple curiosity, an interest in history or something else—shifts into an experience of holiness. This can happen on a conventional tour or in any other kind of travel, and the person is deeply enriched by the shift. The Oxford nun and author Benedicta Ward, in *Pilgrimage of the Heart* (SLG Press, 2001), also refers to the fact that the Christian idea of pilgrimage has always been about more than an outing or a leisure interlude. Rather, it has provided a metaphor for the inner life of Christians since the earliest times, and that metaphor endured, as pilgrimage became an increasingly popular form of devotion throughout the Middle Ages. However, the two concepts of the pilgrim and the tourist were not simple alternatives; they overlapped and drew meaning and resonance from each other. Ward picks up a phrase from one of George Herbert's poems, 'Prayer'—'the heart in pilgrimage'—and sees this as the basic meaning of Christian pilgrimage, whatever form it takes.

In *Sacred Britain* (Piatkus, 1997), Nigel and Martin Palmer point out that most people today never complete the whole of a 'traditional' pilgrimage route, which itself may well have changed over the centuries. All too many of the old paths are now built over or lying under major roads. Many routes were destroyed during the Reformation, when the very idea of pilgrimage was suppressed. Neither do modern pilgrims often use the old modes of travel: cars and coaches have replaced mules and tired feet. Nevertheless, such changes do not undermine the essential nature and blessing of pilgrimage. The journey may now be quicker and easier, the route reinterpreted because of changed terrain, but the fundamental experience is the same. As they travel together to sacred places, pilgrims continue to share and grow in faith and understanding, bringing with them their joys and griefs, their pain and delights, their certainties and doubts. What is of central importance is that they are open to whatever they might discover in the course of the journey.

MOTIVES FOR PILGRIMAGE, THEN AND NOW

Despite all that has been said about the Judeo-Christian roots of pilgrimage, it was not until the medieval period that the experience of Christian pilgrimage came to full flower. It was in the 500-year period leading up to the Reformation (c.1000–1550) that the well-trodden pilgrimage routes became firmly established. Before then, and particularly in the Celtic tradition, Christian monks of the sixth, seventh and eighth centuries were less concerned with travelling to specific holy sites. They were more committed to journeying to unknown places as an act of witness to God—not, strictly speaking, as evangelists but simply as a way of identifying themselves as fellow travellers with God throughout life. By the Middle Ages, several more sophisticated reasons had emerged as to why Christians opted to become pilgrims. It is interesting that many of those early motives continue to encourage people to participate in pilgrimages today.

VISITING THE PLACES WHERE JESUS WAS ACTIVE

Originally, Christians simply wanted to visit the actual places associated with Jesus and some of his close companions. Since the fourth century, when Helena, the mother of the emperor Constantine, believed that she had discovered the true location of Calvary, a steady trickle of pilgrims followed in her footsteps. Consequently, the business of religious travels took a huge leap forward and churches were built over the places where Jesus was believed to have been active; by the eleventh century, pilgrimage routes were clearly marked all over the Holy Land. Rome became a popular place to honour Peter and Paul as well as some of the earliest Christian martyrs. Santiago de Compostela gained prominence as a place where Christians remembered James, and, after the murder of Thomas Becket, Canterbury became a focal point for British pilgrims.

As well as wanting to visit a specific location, early Christians felt a spiritual need to be immersed in the memory of the people associated with these locations. Many of the places of pilgrimage held relics of some of the early saints: pilgrims believed that the relics connected them with the saints, particularly with their prayers as they interceded in God's presence on behalf of the pilgrims, and their perceived power to heal.

FINDING FORGIVENESS

The Celtic idea of pilgrimage almost certainly involved penance, the idea that you had to perform a particular action in order to be rid of a sin. It is generally held that Columba's arrival on Iona from the north of Ireland (c.563) was as a result of an enforced exile in difficult political circumstances, and also as a result of some perceived crime having been committed. Even in this early period, as penitential systems were beginning to be developed for the correction of sin, pilgrimages came to be imposed as a form of penance for certain offences such as theft, adultery and brawling.

By the Middle Ages, the church had firmly established itself as the defender of truth and as the judge of sinful practices. Manuals were written to describe and classify a vast array of differing sins, as well as ways to escape from particular sinful practices. One way was to become a pilgrim and travel to holy places. On the journey, the desire for forgiveness of sins (absolution) and a new start was at the top of the pilgrim's list of reasons for participating. Indeed, the civil courts of the day used the practice as punishment for some crimes (such as minor thefts and complaints against bullies) and some pilgrims even made the journey in chains in order to make the penalty more humiliating.

But this is the stuff of centuries past—or is it? I once led a pilgrimage to Santiago de Compostela and was struck by the queues of people waiting very patiently, sometimes for long periods, to have their 'pilgrim passports' stamped at various places along the route. On arrival at the basilica of St James, they would present their passports again and receive the forgiveness of sins. On another occasion, I was myself a pilgrim at Poland's national shrine of Jasna Góra in Czestochowa, where, along with others, I was invited to crawl on my knees on the hard stone around the high altar sanctuary, which houses the famous icon of the Black Madonna, for forgiveness of any sins that I might have committed over the past year. Like the rest of the pilgrims there, I participated willingly! It is also the case, even today, that at the beginning of a pilgrimage, before a blessing is given for a safe journey, the pilgrim is normally given the opportunity to 'wipe the slate clean' through a particular act of contrition. En route, many modern-day pilgrims feel the urge to open up their hearts to fellow travellers or to the leader and share at a deep level some troubling issue from the past.

RELICS AND SOUVENIRS

As well as creating an awareness of sin (whether by the public exposing of sinners or the process of detailing various sins to a priest), the medieval church was preoccupied with death, hell and judgment. Consequently, increasing numbers of Christians felt the need to seek help to get to heaven and keep out of hell, and this they did through the adoration and kissing of relics and praying to the saints. The collecting of sacred relics or religious souvenirs became an extremely popular medieval hobby. All sorts of body parts were collected in the belief that, as they once belonged to saints, the ongoing prayers of those saints would continue to pour blessings on the new owners of the relics. Seeing, touching and being in the presence of such glimpses of the divine were of paramount importance to the pilgrim.

Some time ago, I was co-leader of an ecumenical pilgrimage to various sites in Spain, including Avila. We shared a very happy celebration of the Eucharist at the convent of La Encarnación, where St Teresa had lived. On our way back to Salamanca, the group were keen to stop at Alba de Tormes, where the saint's elbow is stored in a gold casket. All the members of the group, Catholic and otherwise, queued to see this ancient relic, and I noticed that the group didn't simply look, they also said a prayer. Later that day, there was a chance for the pilgrims to talk about the events of the day and many of them mentioned that it had been the first time they had seen a medieval relic, and told of the inexplicable impact that it had had on them. They didn't want to dismiss it simply as a superstitious remnant of medieval Spanish piety, but neither could many bring themselves to admit that, by seeing the elbow and saying a prayer, they had in some way received a special sense of grace. Yet something deep had happened, and it was best, many of us felt, to leave it at the level of precious mystery.

SEEKING HEALING

Medieval pilgrims often went to pray for the healing of loved ones or to seek healing in their own lives—as people still do today. Praying for a miracle, or a cure that is physical, emotional or psychological, was one of the most common features of pilgrimages, especially if the place of pilgrimage was associated with a saint with a reputation for such miracles. Many specific places—especially holy wells—were connected to particular types of healing, such as for blindness, warts or arthritis. One famous example in Wales is St Winifrede's Well in Holywell, where Beuno (a late sixth-century Welsh missionary priest) built his cell on the site of the present church. Beside the church is the magnificent well, which claims an unbroken line of pilgrimage activity since the seventh century. The twelfth-century Life of Winifrede describes her as Beuno's niece and says that she was born in the early seventh century of noble parents, from whom Beuno obtained land on which to build a church.

One of the most popular pilgrimage churches on the Llyn Peninsula is in the village of Pistyll, and is also dedicated to St Beuno. Although the Christian site here dates back to the sixth century, the present church was built in the twelfth century and lies in a grassy hollow beside a stream, typical of many Welsh coastal chapels that relied on the sea for travel and water for both healing and nourishment. Since it was built, this church has been associated very much with the ministry of healing. It is said that pilgrims on their way to Ynys Enlli (Bardsey Island) would rest at the adjacent monastery, at the inn or at what is still called the 'hospice field', which at that time would have held large huts to accommodate the many sick pilgrims who arrived. This church was noted for the medical care it offered and even has a window known as the 'lepers' window', which lepers could look through and so participate in the worship. Growing on the surrounding hillsides are the offspring of the same herbs and medicinal plants that grew there in the Middle Ages.

TRAVELLING TOGETHER

Another reason why people in the Middle Ages became pilgrims was simply so as to join a group to benefit from each other's company. Chaucer is perhaps most famously remembered for portraying his Canterbury pilgrims entertaining each other and bridging social barriers in a way that would have been difficult under any other circumstance. It was also a dangerous period in which to travel, and journeying in a group made a lot of sense. All over Europe, travellers faced natural hazards—rivers, swamps, mountains. There were also man-made hazards: piracy was a lucrative business at that time, as many pilgrims made at least part of their journey by sea. Pirates pillaged for material wealth as well as for potential slaves. During the early Middle Ages, the 'Knights Templar' and the 'Knights Hospitaller' were founded in order to offer protection to pilgrims not only from professional groups of pillagers but also from the many vagabonds, pickpockets and false guides that awaited travellers along the way.

The desire to travel adventurously in the company of like-minded people, to get away from the familiar and to taste the spiritual delights of what lies elsewhere is as popular today as it was in the Middle Ages. For us, as for the medieval pilgrims, it can be the adventure of a lifetime. Today Christians continue to travel to places where they feel that an encounter between the human and the divine has occurred, and where a certain 'holiness' that was once part of a saint's life continues to encourage and inspire pilgrims.

ADVENTURING IN HOPE

In my many conversations with pilgrims, one thing is clear: pilgrimage is first and foremost a spiritual activity that encourages people from all backgrounds to reach towards God and so to enter into a deeper union with the divine. As such, pilgrims are often given a new awareness of the world they inhabit, a new sense of wonder at aspects of daily life that they had previously taken for granted, a remarkable openness to understanding themselves and others, a sense of adventure into the very heart of God and a glimpse into a new way of being church as fellow pilgrims together. Two contemporary theologians, Craig Bartholomew and Fred Hughes, make the interesting observation (*Explorations in a Christian Theology of Pilgrimage*, Ashgate, 2004) that it is often assumed that journeying to holy places constituted the core meaning of medieval pilgrimage. Their view is that this is not really the case; rather, the primary understanding of pilgrimage that we have inherited from the medieval church is not about journeying to specific sites but about the biblical concept of Christians as pilgrims and strangers who travel through the exile of this world towards heaven.

At the heart of Christian theology lies the crisis of what happened in the garden of Eden. At best, it was a crisis of not hearing God's voice and, at worst, it was one of sheer disobedience. Whichever of these it really was, as a result, human beings have continued as a people in exile—a people who wander the world, feeling remote from God and deprived of a true spiritual home. In many ways, the task of the church down the ages has been to help people recognise that the world is not our true home, and that the whole of life is a pilgrimage from God our Creator back to the arms of God our Father. Pilgrims are those who live with hearts and minds determined to discover more and more of God until they finally enter his presence when this life is over. True pilgrimage is about being transfigured from merely existing in a state of purposeless exile to becoming pilgrims, travelling together towards an ultimate destination.

Modern-day pilgrims are often able to express this idea only in human, rather than faith, terms. Even so, I have encountered many who feel that the very experience of pilgrimage is what has eventually moved them out of a personal situation of exile. We have already defined exile in terms of a deep sense of loss of home, of an authentic place of belonging. Pilgrims move away from this sense of exile by renouncing what they once thought of as 'home' and being willing to journey in search of God's presence in new places. For most of us, this journey will, of course, finally lead us back to a renewed sense of home, but we will find 'home' not to be quite the same place that we originally left, because we have changed as a result of our experiences on the way. The trauma of exile is compounded if we feel we have finally reached what we thought of as 'home' but find instead that we are simply on the next stage of the journey. Pilgrims can get over this disappointment, though, and continue to step out in faith, believing that God must have more to teach them.

CREATING A PROPHETIC CHURCH

If we are indeed living in a world that is out of sync, that swims against the current of God's holiness and God's purposes instead of abiding in his creative and redeeming goodness, this has serious negative consequences not only for ourselves but for the very life of our planet.

Theologically, this is what we mean when we talk in terms of the world living under God's judgment, and getting people to acknowledge this situation was, as we have seen, at the heart of the task facing the biblical prophets. When the prophets' message met with opposition, they reacted by proclaiming hope; as we know only too well, this is a risky business because it has a tendency to provoke critics to anger. But although we live in a world that is under God's judgment, we must never forget that we are also living in one that is under his promise—and recognising this is what truly constitutes the prophetic hope (see Amos 5:14–15; Hosea 2:18–23; Micah 4:1–5; Jeremiah 31:31–34; Isaiah 43:1–5). It would be so much easier for the church today simply to tinker here and there with the status quo: indeed, I believe this is happening in far too many places. The dual task of acknowledging judgment and discovering hope is as urgent as it is risky, but, if the church tackles the task with honesty and courage, it will ultimately expose the world's false promises and ill-gotten certitudes and also start to address properly the overbearing anxiety of so many as to what life's priorities are.

I return to the central message of this book—that the Christian experience of pilgrimage across the world, across traditions and across cultures is a truly prophetic activity that offers a vital way out of the state of exile. I say this because, when I lead pilgrimages, I see a strong determination among participants, particularly as they prepare to return home, to continue to grow into the way of being a truly pilgrim church that they have glimpsed on their journey together. This church is characterised by a deep sense of openness, acceptance, tolerance, forgiveness, creativity and integrity. There are two concepts in particular that encourage pilgrims to move away from a tired and worn model of church and to engage in an emerging prophetic one: seeing all of life as a pilgrimage, and making the link between the inner and outer journeys.

SEEING ALL OF LIFE AS A PILGRIMAGE

I have already said that all of life is a pilgrimage that starts with God and ends with God, and this is demonstrated by a careful reading of the Gospel of Luke in particular. I have often heard preachers declaring that life is a journey from the womb to the grave, and my response is to want to shout out, 'No, it's more than that, even!' Luke begins and ends his Gospel in the temple. At its opening, Zechariah is busy performing his duties in the temple (1:5–10), and we're told that this happened in the very presence of God. Luke is keen to stress that, as the story of Christ unfolds, it will be rooted in that divine presence. At the end of the Gospel, after the resurrection and the ascension, Luke takes his readers back to the temple, where it is now Christ's disciples who continually praise God in that place and do so joyfully (24:50–53). Once again, Luke is careful to root discipleship firmly in God's presence. Before the ascension, Christ blessed the disciples, and now it is we who praise and bless God before dying into life eternal.

Our task, as a pilgrim church, is not simply to focus on short-term strategies to get more people through the doors, but rather to seek the 'heavenly Jerusalem', holding on to the Lukan principle that life starts and ends with God. The pilgrim recognises that as he or she embarks on a journey—say, to Iona—the pilgrim actually has the opportunity to re-enact the whole of his or her life by reimagining it, reliving it and retreading some of its vital steps. Journeying together becomes a means of bringing to mind all of life's insecurities, dangers and disappointments, as well as the joys and blessings.

This task of rediscovery is part of the journey towards heaven. Remembering that, as Luke's Gospel shows us, Christ's life begins in God and returns to God (as do our own lives) gives us a proper sense of perspective as we deal with the uncertainties and difficulties that come our way. Daring to believe that we live under the promise of a creative and redeeming God is a risk, it is true, but ultimately it is the only context in which we can start to create a balanced life. At the same time, we should never forget that the journey and the adventure are never quite done: there is always more to accomplish and more to experience.

THE LINK BETWEEN THE INNER AND THE OUTER JOURNEY

The true pilgrim will always seek a theological context for the pilgrimage experience. Going on a pilgrimage is not a substitute for seeking God in the whole of life; nor is it simply a day out. There is both an inner and an outer journey. The outer journey is what happens visibly and is felt physically as we travel through the days of our lives, and as we go on pilgrimage. The inner journey, on the other hand, is the hidden journey of the heart—those longings and yearnings that cannot be seen but are only held silently by the pilgrim. The physical journey to a sacred place affords us an opportunity to connect both outer and inner journeys and to weave them together—to see the outer 'trip' in some way as a mirror of the inner life. It is only when this connection is made that our relationship with God starts to reach a place of balance and integrity.

By the 16th century, many of the abuses that had crept into the practice of medieval pilgrimage (such as overpaying for indulgences and knowing the right priest at the right time to gain absolution from sin) had been exposed and the practice of pilgrimage began to be banned. Interestingly, it is at this time that we find the outward and often abused trappings of pilgrimage being given a totally new inner meaning. The destruction of the shrines of the saints helped to interiorise the concept of pilgrimage, and what had once been purely materialistic and outer now became richly spiritual and inner. The pilgrim was no longer able to plan a trip to Rome for healing but, instead, was forced to discover what it meant to travel with Christ in a lifetime of self-sacrificial love and service.

＊

—————— *Chapter 6* ——————

WHAT MIGHT HAPPEN ON PILGRIMAGE? JOURNEYING TOGETHER

I never cease to be amazed that something special always happens while I am on pilgrimage. It is usually a small but highly significant thing, like the intimate gelling of particular groups or the little coincidences that people encounter or the word whispered in kindness one to another. But it can also be a bigger issue, such as individuals discovering at last a way of extricating themselves from particularly difficult situations or recognising that they have the personal strength to make significant and life-changing decisions. Whether the issues are big or small, they are all moments of grace.

FINDING OUR PLACE OF RESURRECTION

The way that I like to describe these moments of grace is with the phrase 'finding our own place of resurrection'. By this I mean coming to a situation while on pilgrimage in which a connection is made, or a place is discovered where, in some way, the 'penny drops' and people find a better way to travel forward in their own particular life circumstances. This profound theological idea has been at the heart of the practice of pilgrimage since medieval times.

I first encountered the idea of seeking and finding a personal place of resurrection while reading an English translation of a medieval Welsh poem by Meilyr Brydydd with a group of pilgrims, as we stood on a cliff overlooking Ynys Enlli, which is just off the Llyn Peninsula. Meilyr Brydydd was court poet to Gruffudd ap Cynan, a great prince of Gwynedd during the twelfth century. At that time, the court poets were charged primarily with recording in poetry the achievements of their princes—the equivalent of modern-day tabloid reporters! Towards the end of this particular poem, which is not dedicated to his prince, Meilyr prays that, after his imminent death, he will find his own resurrection on Ynys Enlli. This idea was not original to Meilyr Brydydd, though, and I think it was first used as a personal expression of hope in the writings of Columbanus, the great sixth-century traveller who was responsible for taking the gospel from Ireland to parts of northern Europe via Gaul. He spoke about Christians as 'guests of the world' and about pilgrimage as a process of seeking one's place of resurrection.

In his poem, as he approaches his own death, Meilyr Brydydd pleads for God's mercy and seeks peace and reconciliation with God before he dies. In his pleading, he shows that he is aware of his own fragility and sense of sinfulness (like many modern-day pilgrims, he was at a kind of crossroads point in his own life), and he is determined to renew his commitment to God. He hopes that this renewal will eventually assure him of a good death and a glorious resurrection alongside the 20,000 saints claimed by tradition to be buried on Ynys Enlli. What is particularly interesting is the way in which Meilyr, while seeking and finding his own place of resurrection, also claims that the real, physical island is a means of sanctification—that it can bring people to the point of salvation. He saw Ynys Enlli itself, as an important centre of medieval pilgrimage, in expectation of new life—the head of the island pointing eastwards, as if eagerly awaiting the coming of the risen life, the life of Christ's eternal kingdom.

INTO THE HEART OF THE KINGDOM OF GOD

At the heart of the Christian tradition is the conviction that the children of God already live in this world with one foot in the kingdom of God. In the birth, life, ministry, death and resurrection of Jesus, as recorded in the New Testament, the kingdom of God has already been inaugurated. It is not something that lies entirely in some kind of heavenly future after death; nor is it an experience that can be fully understood and achieved in the here and now. The unfolding of the kingdom of God is both a lifelong experience and a lifelong endeavour that the children of God seek and share with one another and with God himself.

An early, particularly Celtic, interpretation of 'finding a place of resurrection' would have involved discovering an appealingly holy place, either because it was associated with a particular saint or because a divine revelation was believed to have happened there, and imaginatively entering the kingdom of God by journeying to that place. For some early thinkers, this holy place became the divinely appointed location where the pilgrim seeker would settle and spend the rest of life—whether that was a matter of weeks, months or years—in a state of penance and anticipation. In an immediate sense, it was simply a waiting room en route to the eventual place of resurrection; it would be the threshold of heaven. This is the background to understanding and appreciating Meilyr Brydydd's love of Ynys Enlli.

The connection, therefore, between particular sacred places, the practice of pilgrimage and the theological idea of finding a place of resurrection is a crucially important one. As we have already seen, generations of Christians have known that pilgrimage is not simply a vaguely religious holiday with a bit of worship thrown in. Rather, it is a journey where the destination itself is sacred—and standing in one of these holy destinations of resurrection helps pilgrims to perceive something of the resurrection possibilities for their own lives. Remembering this is essential for grasping the depth of participation and commitment that true pilgrimage requires. As a pilgrimage leader, I have seen how particular places become powerful anchors of faith. This first came home to me when I was a young student visiting Jerusalem. Someone had told me to walk up the Mount of Olives at 5a.m. to see the sun rise, because then I would understand the meaning of 'Jerusalem the Golden'. I did as suggested and, when I arrived at the top, I found several young men there already, holding their babies and whispering into their ears. I was astonished! As I got closer, I realised that they were in fact whispering parts of the Hebrew scriptures: those young fathers clearly knew the place and they were keen for their tiny babies to begin knowing the story in the hope that they would eventually come to know God. The disciples' vision of the resurrected Jesus (John 21; Luke 24) revealed to them not only the glory of God but also what it meant to be most fully human. The greatest surprise of the resurrection was that, in seeing the risen Christ, the disciples saw themselves anew. They realised that they had actually participated in and witnessed the most powerful of all the episodes of history and were determined to pass on the story and the opportunity for others (including us) to experience it.

Immersed, then, in the complexity and mess of human living today, what are we to make of all this? What exactly does the idea of 'finding a place of resurrection' mean to us today? My experience with pilgrims convinces me that to speak in medieval terms of seeking holy places in order to lay down our heads in a kind of sacred penance and patient waiting for death would be to miss the mark entirely. In my view, talk about seeking a place of resurrection in the contemporary context means three interrelated truths.

EXPLORING LIFE'S PRIORITIES

The first truth is the most basic and human of them all. Journeying together as pilgrims to a particular holy place affords us a vital opportunity to reflect on what is really important in our lives and to examine our priorities in order to establish three things: a faithful stability in terms of our relationship with each other, with God and with ourselves; an authentic security in terms of generally feeling secure about life and comfortable with who and what we are personally; and, ultimately, a well-balanced lifestyle. Far too many people in our so-called comfortable and developed societies live frantic and frenetic lifestyles, unable to find contentment and true anchorage. Pausing, either alone or with others, along the pilgrim way to reflect on what it means to be truly human can be challenging—even frightening—because we are confronted with the depth and realities (or otherwise) of our personal identities.

The legacy of the early saints associated with many of these pilgrim ways continues to be twofold. First, in their time, these saints drew out the sacredness of the land we walk on today. In other words, they identified certain places that showed them how God's presence could be discerned there. Second, they enable us to use our own experience of that sacredness to make some crucial connections, to recognise some of those times when the journey of the heart and the physical pilgrimage of life coincide—the inner and outer journeys that we mentioned previously. To have found our own place of resurrection is, I think, the moment when the connection is made between a particular experience of life, whether bitter or sweet, and God. I have seen, over the years, how pilgrim places become places of resurrection because it is there that pilgrims find relinquishment or reconciliation or renewal. Pausing as pilgrims in places such as Iona, Glendalough and Holy Island helps them mentally to release the mother dying back home, or reconsider a broken relationship, or rethink a career, or reclaim a long-lost family member, or rediscover a sense of stability in their life. Even if we have not, as yet, found our own place of resurrection, a pilgrimage can lead to a chance of imagining the possibility of a new life, new beginnings, new perspectives—to take hold of or start to seek a place of resurrection. It's worth remembering, of course, that actually finding that place of resurrection can come as a complete surprise to many people—an unlooked-for and unexpected 'moment of grace'.

THE PILGRIM PATH IS LOCATED EVERYWHERE

The second truth linked to finding a place of resurrection in a contemporary context is that while places such as St Davids, Durham, Lindisfarne and Canterbury are, in different ways, very much associated with traditional pilgrimage, in reality the true pilgrim path is located everywhere and is never confined to conventional 'sacred spaces'. The question that faces every pilgrim—indeed, every Christian—is always: am I open to being truly a pilgrim? Am I prepared to live with some of the risks and uncertainties and loose ends that pilgrimage always entails? The pilgrim can never have everything neatly 'sewn up'. There is always the exploration, the search, the movement, the questions, the challenge and the surprise—and these are the very stuff of both life and resurrection. In this sense, finding a place of resurrection is about allowing space for the unlikely, the unlooked for and the extraordinary to happen. One of the biggest gifts of the first Easter Sunday was the surprise that it gave to the women who came to the grave early to seek their Lord. A carefully ordered and regimented way of life can leave precious little space for God's surprises to break in. In our finding of places of resurrection, it is imperative that we allow time and space through which God's whisper and God's constant longing to surprise us can be heard and experienced.

I was once on a pilgrimage to St Catherine's Monastery in Sinai, travelling from Jerusalem with a small group of theological students. We'd been told that the journey was going to be long and arduous and we had planned the route carefully, organising our travel first by bus, then in jeeps and finally on camels. That journey was the moment when I discovered the importance of travelling light—not just in Sinai but throughout life. Had I been tempted by clutter, the whole journey would have been a disaster. Similarly, had we not allowed time and space for mistakes and serious delays, then we would have been disappointed. Because we travelled simply and lightly, Sinai was a great joy. Those who approach the whole of life in this way are the ones who are able to face it with joy and hope and regard it all as a precious gift.

THE GIFT OF PILGRIMAGE

Thirdly, whether the places to which pilgrims journey are places of silence and prayer, of beauty and light, of imaginative transition from this world to the next, or even of noise and the busyness of human life and longing, they are all places where we can receive a precious and irreplaceable gift. They are doors through which we can catch a glimpse of another world—or, better, perhaps, through which another world may reach us. There is in these places at least a presence of the past, but also a presence of eternity demanding both our reverence and gratitude. Ultimately, it is this third aspect of resurrection places and resurrection surprises that we strive for the most, and may well be blessed to discover while on pilgrimage.

For each one of us the journey will be different, and the route towards tomorrow and towards our own place of resurrection—whether in the sense of seeking balance and authenticity in this life or in the ultimate sense of seeking the glory of heaven—is one that we must each discover for ourselves. Although it is a unique path that faces each of us, it is nevertheless not a solitary one. Journeying alongside others is always an experience of sharing and learning together. The gift of true pilgrimage is that, by arriving at our physical destinations, we are often surprised to find that the joys and the hopes, the grief and the anguish of our own lives have already been experienced by the people who made those places sacred in the first place. It is often their example and their abiding company, the communion of saints, that point us forward to tomorrow and fill us with the hope that we too will come to experience resurrection for ourselves.

Part 4

… if I exalt not Jerusalem above my dearest joy.

PSALM 137:6

✳

Chapter 7

PLACES OF PILGRIMAGE: VISITS AND CHALLENGES

At the beginning of this book we considered the fact that far too many Christian communities are on the verge of forgetting the story of God's creative and redeeming work. We also considered how pilgrimage offers a way to reverse this process of forgetting. In the final part of the book, I'm going to share eight stories of visiting significant places of pilgrimage, along with the stories of people I encountered there and something of the effect the pilgrimage had on their lives. Although I've disguised individual names, their life stories and the impact that the place had on them are all true. Through this, we will start to see how places of pilgrimage can help us to remember the Christian story anew and contribute to our search for a deeper experience of the kingdom of God.

My encounters with these people helped me to recognise the importance in Christian spirituality of distinguishing between the act of remembering and simply being nostalgic. Nostalgia is no more than going back over the past to provoke a particular emotional response, usually sentimental and often involving a sense of loss. Remembering is a wholly different experience: it's a deliberate bringing to mind and an essential part of the process of acknowledging what has actually happened in our lives. Philip Sheldrake has written extensively about pilgrimage and about the spirituality of place, and he goes as far as saying that remembering is vital to a healthy sense of identity. He also makes the point that to forget is an act of exoneration and excuse where neither reconciliation nor forgiveness can be found ('Space and the sacred: cathedrals and cities', *Contact* 147, 2005).

As Christians, we know about the importance of the process of remembering only too well. Whatever our spiritual tradition— whether it be Catholic, Orthodox, Anglican or Reformed—as we participate in the Eucharist, for instance, we recognise that it's not an act of nostalgia but something much more profound. For many of us, it is difficult to find words to interpret this recognition and articulate what it means for our individual lives. Far too often, many of us make a mess when we try to describe it in words but I think it's about recollecting the detail of what went on in the upper room that Thursday evening before Good Friday. It's about recalling the way in which the Church over the centuries has tried to make sense of what happens when Christians gather together to make their communion. It's about revisiting the impact that the presence of the risen Christ had on Cleopas and his companion as they walked to Emmaus early that Sunday evening and broke bread together. None of this is nostalgia but all of it is a powerful act of true remembrance.

Again, Philip Sheldrake makes a fascinating observation, that the Eucharist makes space for unheard stories to be told and for suffering to be redressed. For him, the Eucharist is a place of reconciliation, somewhere that makes space for memories that refuse to remain silent (*Spaces for the Sacred*, SCM, 2001). I agree wholeheartedly but would add that many of the traditional pilgrimage sites are places of reconciliation in a similar way.

The stories that I'm going to relate are about pilgrims seeking healing in their lives for all sorts of different reasons, pilgrims searching for space to be healed through the conscious act of remembering their own stories in relation to Christ. In sharing with them, I saw how the act of remembering is often very painful, particularly if it involves admitting the truth of a situation or relationship for the first time. Such an act forces us to put aside any kind of nostalgic sentimentality and is an essential part of any process of healing. These pilgrims discovered a new sense of purpose and perspective precisely as they paused to remember their own stories at particular places: they found a way of coming to terms with the past. Is this not what happened to the disciples at the tomb early that Sunday morning?

Until they came to the place of the tomb and found it empty, they remained in a state of devastation. For them, as for many of us, resurrection is possible only when we start at the tomb. It is not really possible to discover a place of resurrection, of healing, of personal repair that releases us from our own loss, if we do not admit that loss in the first place. In this way the empty tomb of Christ becomes yet another metaphor that allows us to discover a place to start again. Ultimately, as in Jerusalem during those three astonishing days over 2000 years ago, healing and resurrection are a work of God and a moment of grace, which may not be at the time or place of our choosing, although we can seek it faithfully as pilgrims. Such a moment of grace comes about through God's breaking into our lives, either to precipitate a process of healing or to show us where we should seek it.

THE SIGNIFICANCE OF PLACE

Pilgrimage has always involved a strong attachment to place. The true pilgrim is one who consciously embarks on a journey to a specific holy place which can have an impact on that pilgrim's life simply because of the revelation of God associated with that place. The significance of place is therefore central in the journey to remembering our story. In cultures across the world, physical geography is often understood both symbolically and spiritually. Indeed, for many people, part of the unique quality of their culture and traditions is symbolised by the land and particular places in that land. This powerful fact struck me when I first visited the

Holy Land as a student and then, in later years, as a pilgrim and a pilgrimage leader. Reading the Gospels there showed me that both the landscape itself and specific locations within it have been given a great deal of theological and spiritual significance over the generations. Understanding the Gospels involves not only remembering who and what Jesus really was, but also that he lived in a particular land and the impact that specific places in the land had upon him and the development of the early Church.

On one occasion, I was part of a group of pilgrims travelling from Jerusalem to Galilee, and we made a slight detour in order to visit Mount Gerizim and a Samaritan temple that still operated in that area. We stopped for coffee at Nablus and visited Jacob's well. At the well, I was asked by the pilgrimage leader to read the relevant passage from John's Gospel (4:5–26), which is the account of Jesus' encounter with the Samaritan woman at that very same well. So that the whole group could hear me clearly, I sat on the well itself. It brought the story to extraordinary and vivid life because that was exactly where the story first happened: countless Christians over the ages have paused there to listen to that story again and now here I was reading it to yet another group of Christians. The experience brought home to me the fact that the Jesus described in the Gospels is a man who belonged not only to a particular time but also to a particular place, and that 'place' has powerful significance in people's lives.

To overlook the emphasis on particular places in the Gospels is, in fact, to overlook one of the most persistent and passionately held beliefs in the whole of the Bible. In the Old Testament, for instance, the idea that Israel is the centre of the world and a truly holy place is common (Ezekiel 5:5; 38:12). Similarly, religious communities right across the world would lay some kind of claim to their own land—wherever it is—as having spiritual and holy significance; for them, it is somehow a symbol of the cosmos. The relationship between a people, a land and their God is what ultimately offers orientation, security and comfort.

In biblical language, the words for 'place' (*maqom* in Hebrew, and *topos* or *chora* in Greek) describe places where events of human and divine significance have occurred—a dwelling place, a place of meeting, a site for gathering together. In the Hebrew sense, to lose one's place is actually to cease to be. In the biblical tradition, therefore, place is an integral aspect of individual and national existence—hence the catastrophic nature of the whole exile experience.

Interestingly, the author of Psalm 90 refers to God as our place of existence or dwelling. Here it's not the case that the world is God's dwelling place but rather the reverse: God is the dwelling place of the world. The psalmist suggests that all places discover their true meaning through their rootedness in God. This resonates with what we considered earlier about life as a pilgrimage, beginning and ending in God as our ultimate place of dwelling.

The New Testament does not ignore these passionately held convictions about holy places. Although, in many ways, the trajectory of the New Testament transcends land and place—moving from Jerusalem and temple into the world—its history and theology continue to demand a special concern for these realities. In one sense, the New Testament finds holy places wherever Christ has been; it personalises holy place in Christ, who, as a man of history, was nevertheless rooted in the land. At the same time, for the holiness of place the New Testament fundamentally substitutes the holiness of the person of Christ and hallows places by connecting them directly with his life. After the resurrection, the concept of holy places takes on a new significance because such places are now touched in some way by the presence of the risen Christ, through the life and witness of those faithful people who have followed him down the ages.

PLACES OF CALL AND CONVERSION

The biblical tradition also shows us that people are generally called beyond the holy place of initial encounter to meet God in other places as well. In his pastoral ministry in Babylon, Jeremiah warns the people of Israel, now in exile, not to associate God exclusively with the temple many hundreds of miles away in Jerusalem. He points out that the divine presence can even be encountered on foreign ground in Babylon (Jeremiah 29:7). Similarly, in the New Testament Peter wants to erect three tents on Mount Tabor—one for Jesus, one for Moses and one for Elijah—so that they can all stay as long as possible to savour the experience of transfiguration. Jesus refuses to comply and instead encourages his disciples to follow him down the mountain so as to get on with the messy business of human living (Mark 9:2–8). After the resurrection, he encourages his followers to move beyond Jerusalem and make their way to the ends of the earth as his true witnesses (Acts 1:8).

The realities surrounding the significance of place in Christian thinking are complex. There appears to be a continuing tension between the particular place and a moving onwards from that place. It is the case that God is present on Iona, Ynys Enlli and Lindisfarne but, at the same time, God is not only there: he cannot be limited exclusively to particular places, however holy they appear to be. In a challenging article about the role of cathedrals today, Christopher Lewis, Dean of Christ Church, Oxford, points out that an important ingredient often missing in the contemporary pilgrimage experience is the emphasis on returning home ('The risen Lord and the liberation of place', *Contact* 147, 2005). He believes that it is, of course, possible that the risen Christ can be encountered in particular holy places, but the point of the destination is to move pilgrims ever onwards. Just as in the account of the transfiguration, an experience of mountain-top ecstasy is not meant to last for ever. Christopher Lewis warns us against hanging around obsessively at specific sites: the challenge of the destination is that pilgrims are to continue to journey, renewed in their faith, so as to continue witnessing to God's creative and redeeming work in the world.

I think this is what Augustine of Hippo was trying to encapsulate in his commentary on Psalm 122, which emphasised the metaphorical value of pilgrimage and the fact that the Christian is one who is always striving for better—for healing, maybe. Augustine wrote that his pastoral experience among Christians was that so many of them 'groan' and find life a heavy burden, even when all is going well. It seems that things were not so different in fifth-century North Africa, where Augustine served as a bishop, from what they are in 21st-century Europe! Augustine's remedy for his people's groaning was to encourage them to strive onwards as pilgrims, not to be static but to keep walking. For him, the pains and the longings of the people would lead them to sing the words of the psalm: 'I lift my eyes to you, to you who have your home in heaven' (Psalm 123:1).

DESTINATIONS

Having said all this, we should bear in mind a key point about pilgrimage destinations made by John Inge, Bishop of Worcester and a specialist in the study of the theology of place. While the whole journey is important, from preparation right through to the return home, at the end of the day the actual destination does have—must have—a central role to play. He says that an exclusive concentration on the journey 'skews the perfect balance which pilgrimage allows' ('A tale of two cities and the genius of pilgrimage', The Reader, 2008).

It remains true that any pilgrimage is about the process of preparation before setting off, the sharing of the journey for a while with fellow travellers along the way, and all the practical realities involved with modern-day travel. At the same time, the arrival at the point of destination is a quintessential part of the whole experience. It means arriving somewhere, as Inge says, where the divine/human encounter has worked itself into the story and fabric of the place itself. The spiritual writer and theologian Donald Allchin puts it in yet another way, that these are 'places of God's epiphany'. They reveal sheer beauty and holiness through the lives of those who have either lived or prayed constantly there—people who have been particularly open to God's epiphany (*The World Is a Wedding*, DLT, 1978).

These places of epiphany are also places where some rather remarkable things have taken place. One writer who has influenced my own thinking on the spirituality of place almost more than any other is the American academic Belden Lane. He claims—rightly, I think—that throughout the history of Christianity, place and spirituality belong together (*The Solace of Fierce Landscapes*, OUP, 1998). For so many of the great figures of Christian spirituality, the experience of God was also an experience of place—Kevin's Glendalough, Becket's Canterbury, Columba's Iona, Cuthbert's Lindisfarne, Ninian's Whithorn and Cadfan's Ynys Enlli. For all of them, an intimate part of the spiritual truth that shaped their lives was encountered in those particular places.

It is also interesting to notice the way in which the Christian tradition anchors very detailed experiences in the memory of specific places so as to recall and describe vivid encounter between God and his people. We remember Paul and the road to Damascus, Constantine and the Milvian Bridge, Augustine and a garden in Milan, John Wesley and London's Aldersgate Street, Bonhoeffer and Tegel prison. Belden Lane makes the point that, for all these people, the place itself lent an essential structure, a significant context and a vividness of memory to their spiritual story.

HOW DOES IT AFFECT ME?

At the heart of all this lies the 'So what?' question. As a parish priest, I find that this question crops up time and again. Over the years I have come to recognise that it is, in fact, one of the most important pastoral and spiritual questions, one that the church should be encouraging her people to ask to make sense of the story of faith. Whatever the celebration, be it Christmas, Easter, Pentecost, harvest, a saint's day or a normal Sunday morning, Christians should be asking, 'So what? How has this particular celebration changed me? What impact has it had on me? Have I been influenced in any significant way through this celebration? What difference will it make as I continue with daily life?' If we fail to see the relevance of the 'So what?' question for us as individuals, then our worship will simply be a lesson in history rather than an authentic experience of the risen Christ.

Similarly, the 'So what?' question is a vital one for pilgrims, who are urged at every level to reflect theologically on what is happening within and around them. As we travel together to so-called 'thin places', where the closeness between heaven and earth can be much more easily encountered and where all sorts of human experiences—bitter and sweet—can find a place to be remembered, we always carry with us the story of Christ. In Philip Sheldrake's words, the Christian community carries this salvation story, culminating in the empty tomb, which subverts all our human places and moves us towards the unnameable presence that we call 'God'. Our journeys to these special places do not simply make us better people but push us onwards as life pilgrims towards the God in whom our whole life journey originally began.

─────────── *Chapter 8* ───────────

GLENDALOUGH: FINDING GOD AT THE EDGE

MICHAEL

Michael had always been a grade A student and was both intelligent and popular: he was always the first to be picked for the football team. He had a good start in life and one that some would describe as privileged. He had an equally popular and bright sister, and parents with successful careers in teaching. They were quite an affluent family and Michael and his sister were always able to take advantage of school trips abroad. After A Levels, Michael headed off to university, where he was once again successful and well liked by his peers. After graduation, his life and his career took off in a brilliant direction: in many ways his beginnings had been perfect.

Although Michael was away from home during his three years at university, most of his weekends and all of his holidays were spent at home, as he was close to his parents and liked to be surrounded by old friends. He continued to play for his home town football team and preferred the social life there rather than at college. As a result, he had not really made a break with home, but eventually the time came when he had to move away to seek work. Just before he left for London, Michael's father arranged an extravagant family holiday abroad and they enjoyed a great time together. One of the things that they talked about was the importance of a good start in life—a bit like having a hearty breakfast at the beginning of the day. Michael and his sister expressed their gratitude for the good start they had had, but Michael didn't quite appreciate what his parents were actually saying. In truth, they were rather worried—worried for themselves, that their lives were now going to change, and worried for Michael. How would he cope with life outside the family circle?

Michael got a good job in a bank and everything seemed to be going well. But gradually he began to feel under tremendous pressure as 'going it alone' in a large impersonal city took its toll on him. He started to feel lonely, and in the aloneness he found himself having to confront who this person called Michael really was. The process unnerved him and he began to lose confidence, particularly as he came to realise that, for quite a long time, his whole life had been managed for him by his loving but perhaps overprotective parents. In many ways he had been living through them, doing what he thought they wanted him to do. He was now scared at the prospect—the real possibility—of disappointing his family and his colleagues at work and seriously failing, for the first time ever. He just couldn't seem to get his act together and find the confidence that he had once enjoyed so freely.

I met Michael on the ferry sailing back to Holyhead from Dun Laoghaire. I had been in Dublin for a three-day summer school with the clergy of the diocese of Bangor. It was a particularly rough journey and I found myself sitting at a table with a group of strangers. Michael was one of them and the book he was reading caught my eye: it was aimed specifically at pilgrims visiting Glendalough (*Glendalough: A Celtic Pilgrimage*, Michael Rodgers and Marcus Losack, Columba, 1996). It seemed appropriate at least to begin a conversation with this young man because, two days before, I, along with about 30 other clerics, had made a day's pilgrimage to Glendalough under the leadership of Michael Rodgers. His eyes lit up as he told me that he too had been to Glendalough for three days, and we then chatted about our respective pilgrimages for the rest of the journey to Holyhead. The conversation meant that we no longer noticed the storm outside.

SEEKING PLACES OF SOLITUDE

Kevin is probably the second best-known saint of Ireland, Patrick being the first, and it is Kevin who is reputed to have founded Glendalough as a Christian site when he established a small monastery there, some time during the late sixth century. At an early age he was sent to a monastery in Dublin, where he studied theology under three spiritual guides: Eogan, Lochan and Erna. Eventually, after visiting other monasteries, he decided to locate himself permanently in Glendalough. At first, he shared his life with other monks in the vicinity of what is known as Glendalough's Lower Valley. However, he was increasingly drawn to a life of solitude and moved up the valley, where he found himself a cell in a cave between the lake and the mountain and lived there for the rest of his life as a hermit and Christian mystic.

This urge by early Christians to seek God at a more profound level characterises many of the pilgrimage places I have visited. Holy men and women established religious communities, only to find that God then called them to move on to a place of greater solitude. The model for this is the experience of many Christians in the third and fourth centuries in the deserts of northern Egypt—men and women leaving places of busyness and activity to seek the silence of the desert in order to encounter the divine. As already mentioned, I once participated in a pilgrimage to Sinai, travelling across the desert towards St Catherine's Monastery. The journey took us the best part of four days and we spent each night in the open desert under the stars.

During one of those nights, I remembered a short poem by Christopher Logue that I had read to pilgrims on a previous occasion back home in Wales. Entitled 'Come to the edge', it describes the fear of stepping into the unknown. When the step is taken, however, the experience is one of exhilaration rather than fear—of flying rather than falling.

The desert is certainly a place 'on the edge' of everything—a place that transgresses the limits of culture, language and the personal boundaries by which our lives are framed and controlled.

Travelling together for days in the desert stretched us, as pilgrims, to our personal limits, but as a group we recognised that coming to a place that feels like the edge helps to force a breakthrough to something and somewhere that is beyond all previously conceived thresholds. This must have been what attracted the early Christians to abandon all the comforts they may have had and to risk becoming part of one of the most exciting spiritual experiments in the whole of Christian history. They had the opportunity to discover a new way of life that could not be taught in a church but was, rather, something they caught through association with other like-minded spiritual risk-takers. It was risky precisely because there was no model of the way others had done it. The early Desert Fathers and Mothers (as they became known) had the hard task of redirecting every aspect of body, mind and soul towards God in search of the closest possible encounter with the divine.

JESUS' PLACES ON THE EDGE

Although there was no direct biblical blueprint as to how this way of life should be developed, the Gospels do offer an insight into its significance in the life of Jesus. At the very beginning of Mark's Gospel, Jesus is driven to the desert. The original Greek word used in Mark 1:12 to convey the sense of being driven (literally 'thrust forth') to the desert means that Jesus was forced to take the hard way—going directly from his baptism into the wilderness for a period of 40 days. It's worth noting, too, the way Matthew's Gospel takes up the importance of 'edge-places' in Jesus' life. As for so many of the biblical writers, Matthew's edge-place is primarily the mountain. He begins on the mountain of temptation (Matthew 4), where Jesus refuses to take the easy way, and gradually moves his readers on to the mountain of commissioning in Galilee at the end of the Gospel, where Jesus declares to his disciples that all power in heaven and on earth has now been given to him (28:16–20).

Set between these two mountains, which form the backdrop to the opening and closing of Matthew's Gospel, are four other mountains that reveal Jesus' unique nature and calling. The first is the mount of the Beatitudes, where he teaches the new radical ethic of the kingdom (Matthew 5—7). Then comes the mountain on which 5000 people are fed and Jesus prefigures the messianic banquet of that kingdom (14:13–21). The mount of the transfiguration reveals Jesus as anticipating his absolute glory (17:1–8) and on the Mount of Olives he describes the end time and the final revelation of God's kingdom (ch. 24).

On each of these mountains, these Gospel edge-places, an established order is broken down, a family is formed, new rules are adopted and Jesus repeatedly leads his people to the edge, a place that is always different and risky. Now, as then, Jesus invites us into a place that is altogether new, just as he took his disciples from the familiarity of home and those trappings that only poorly imitated security, while all the time declaring the true power of the kingdom.

THE EMERGENCE OF CHRISTIAN MONASTICISM

Eventually the wilderness of Judea and the deserts of northern Egypt became the thriving hub of the newly emerging Christian monastic world. Christians came from all over the Byzantine empire—Syria, Mesopotamia, Cappadocia, Armenia and even beyond—to seek solitude in these places. Gradually they established two kinds of monastic groups. The first, which was the more typical form of early Palestinian monasticism, was that of the 'Laura', a cluster of solitary cells round a common centre, including a church and a bakery, where the monks would assemble on Saturdays and Sundays, spending the rest of the week in their cells. The second form was the 'Coenobium', which was far more communal. This was more characteristic of the Nile Delta, and such sites developed as important training places for young Christians.

For the followers of both these forms of monasticism, the geographical link with the places associated with the life of Christ was significant. The spiritual activity of these wilderness and desert Christians was always overshadowed by Bethlehem and Jerusalem—the cities of the incarnation and redemption. In their quest for the eternal and the ultimate, they were never far removed from that which links the life of faith to time and history. Herein, I think, lies the very core of the vocation to the monastic life, indeed the vocation to the whole of Christian life. It was, and still is, a call to live firmly in the tension of witnessing both to the eternal Father and to the Word incarnate in history.

Perhaps this tension is also expressed as an awareness that, although our redemption has been completed in Christ and the benefits imparted to us through baptism, we have as yet only a glimpse of the glory of the final fulfilment of Christ's kingdom. The chief aim of these early desert Christians was to seek the edge in order to discover the true depth of life, where God is all in all—a sign to the rest of the Christian community of the continual inbreaking of the kingdom of God.

GLENDALOUGH

As time elapsed, more and more Christians from the west travelled to see what was happening in the desert, and this exciting spiritual experiment spread to Gaul (France) and then to Britain and Ireland. Kevin was one of those who became hooked on the new religious lifestyle, and Glendalough emerged as his place on the edge. Almost certainly, a group of sixth-century Christians gathered around Kevin, their teacher, who were willing to take some spiritual risks and experiment with the eastern ways of prayer, worship and contemplation that they had heard about.

It wasn't until Kevin died in 618 that pilgrims began making their way to Glendalough, believing that they could thereby obtain as much remission from their sins as by a single visit to Rome. The pilgrim route to Glendalough was, like so many others, peppered with small crosses, stones and churches, and many of these can still be seen today, such as the one on the Laragh–Glendalough road. Traditionally pilgrims gathered at this point to pray before entering Glendalough, probably offering a prayer of thanksgiving for a safe journey and seeking God's blessing on arrival at the holy place.

By the twelfth century, Glendalough had become an important diocese in its own right, known as 'the Monastic City' and an excellent example of an early Celtic monastery. Just as early Christians in the east were drawn to the desert, so the Irish were drawn to this small, isolated and rural place and transformed it into a place directly under the rule of God, where the kingdom was made manifest and its members were citizens of heaven. The boundary around Glendalough marked the division between a secular and a sacred space: in the sacred, the rule of God was paramount and those seeking refuge were welcomed and protected. Tradition preserves the memory of Glendalough as a healing sanctuary associated with miracles, cures and resurrection—truly a place to discover transformation in life.

Within the boundary, all kinds of activities would have taken place—writing, painting, education, agriculture, metalwork, tanning and regular daily worship. The Monastic City would have contained a hospital, a bakery, a kitchen, a library, a scriptorium and, of course, space for hospitality. All of these would have been built around the more central buildings—the cathedral, the abbot's house, the guesthouse and the round tower for protection.

By the Middle Ages, Glendalough had become a significant place of pilgrimage. During this period, travelling from Ireland to Rome and Jerusalem would have been extremely dangerous and difficult, and Glendalough became one of the four great pilgrimage sites of Ireland—the others being Croagh Patrick, Lough Derg and Skellig Michael. Today's pilgrim is invited to explore the site of the monastic community and visit the many impressive ancient ruins—the gateway, the round tower, the cathedral, the abbot's house, St Kevin's church, St Ciaran's church, the Lady church, Trinity church, St Saviour's church, Reefert church, St Kevin's cell and St Kevin's bed.

CEILE DE

One of the most interesting contemporary features of the Christian spiritual life in Glendalough is the Ceile De group, an ecumenical organisation specialising in the development of study programmes, pilgrimages and resources in the Celtic tradition.

Ceile De is the historic name of a spiritual reform movement that sought to return to the teachings of the desert and contributed to the flowering of Celtic art, calligraphy and spiritual formation during the so-called golden age of Celtic Christianity (c.500–1000). It was chosen as the name of the modern-day initiative to show solidarity with the aims of those in the past who were an inspiration to the movement, and to rekindle the fire and vision of the Celtic tradition for today. It was some of the Ceile De literature that Michael was reading on the ferry back to Wales on the day I met him.

TRANSFORMATION

In the course of my conversation with Michael, I told him that I had been to Glendalough many times. The first time was when I was a student in Dublin, when I first came across the modern Ceile De group and its founder, Marcus Losack. Since then I have returned with several pilgrimage groups. Michael related part of his life story to me and said that one of his colleagues, originally from Cork in southern Ireland, had suggested he take a holiday in Dublin, plus, possibly, a few reflective days in Glendalough. Michael had thought this would be good and proceeded to make the arrangements—and I met him as we were both on our way home.

I was interested to learn more about the effect his pilgrimage to Glendalough had had on him, as he was clearly at an important crossroads in his life. I had picked up from our conversation that he found it difficult to live in what was, to him, a large and very impersonal city, and this was a major contributory factor to his feeling generally ill at ease. His loneliness had forced him to travel inwards, and in his internal journey he had had to confront who and what he really was—a young man lacking confidence and personal strength, who had been propped up by doting parents for too long and was scared of disappointing family and close friends. But I noticed that he spoke in the past tense: clearly he had made a significant discovery in Glendalough.

FINDING STRENGTH

As you wander around the impressive ruins of Glendalough, you get the impression that St Kevin had achieved great things. Not only had he discovered a holy place—or, at least, brought into the Christian sphere an already existing popular place of sanctity; he had also managed to gather around himself a group of dedicated followers, because he was a born leader. But he let all of this go and headed for the solitary life in a cell. Kevin's life story is preserved in several early writings, the earliest being a Latin version, the Codex Kilkenniensis. His story relates how he was a gentle, loving and kind person, with an extraordinary and unusual affinity to nature, especially birds and animals.

It is quite possible that although Kevin took the initial step in establishing Glendalough, he was not the one to develop it further and he needed to be honest about his own capabilities. His story relates the courage with which he headed for a place of solitude in order to know who and what he really was and to find a place at life's edge in order to develop his strength and endurance. Kevin chose the hard way: he built his cell on the dark side of Glendalough's upper lake, which remains in shadow for almost six months of the year. He opted to expose himself in this way so as to test himself to the limit and, through that testing, to find the fullness of his own strengths.

St Kevin's cell can still be visited today but with great care, as it is one of Glendalough's least accessible places. The path to the cell is dangerous—steep and at times almost vertical, a reminder of the difficult inner journey to life's more profound places. Kevin chose that journey, and his path through years of contemplation led him deep into the mystery of God. When Michael came to Glendalough on pilgrimage, he was keen to spend some time at this place and pause for a while to think about his own life. He told me how ascending the flight of steps reminded him of the flight of his own life and all the steps he had travelled from home to college and to what had become, for him, an unbearable life.

All that is left of the old cell are a few of the original foundation stones. But, as well as those stones, there continues to be an atmosphere of intense and precious stillness, and it was this that struck Michael. He told me how, in that stillness, he simply acknowledged God and felt strongly that God acknowledged him as he was. In this way, Michael had come to a greater acceptance of who and what he really was, for the first time. Finally, he related how he had read that three oak trees had been growing close to the cell for many years, like three strong spirits protecting the cell. Today, one of those trees is dying, and Michael was encouraged to read that the dying tree may well represent all those people who are starved of authentic living through lack of space to be truly themselves, and the stillness to know themselves in a crowded and noisy world.

At last Michael had found in Glendalough the space he needed to know and be himself. It had been a greatly rewarding pilgrimage for him: I got the impression that God had asked him to come to this edge and, when he accepted the invitation, God pushed him gently and he discovered his own way of flying.

＊

LOUGH DERG: A FRESH START

VICTORIA

Victoria was a withdrawn woman in her mid-40s who always came to church late. She didn't play any kind of active role in the congregation but attended for reasons best known to herself. She had tried her hand at several jobs but couldn't settle, and some said that she'd had several sweethearts but couldn't keep them either. She was one of those people who walked with an odd kind of limp, as if she had something heavy weighing her down.

When she was a teenager, Victoria's parents had encouraged her to go to a technical college quite close to home in order to gain secretarial skills. She agreed to go but never completed the course. About halfway through the first year, she met a young man called John and they began a relationship. They appeared to be a happy couple and enjoyed various joint activities—walking, cinema and stamp collecting. They even visited each other's homes and both sets of parents were pleased with the couple. They also had much in common: both of them came from quite conservative Christian backgrounds, both were only children and both were very shy.

One night they had been invited to a party to celebrate a college friend's birthday. Neither of them was used to alcohol—Victoria actually didn't like it—but after far too much wine they went back to John's place, where things got seriously out of hand. With too much alcohol already in his system, John decided to indulge in a nightcap and became sexually aroused. Three months prior to this, both he and Victoria had decided that their relationship was not going to be sexual and that they preferred to wait until they could make a serious commitment to one another. That night, John felt that the time had come but Victoria disagreed. John forced himself on her and Victoria was raped. She never quite recovered from that tragedy and withdrew almost completely from any close relationships for several years.

It was the shock of her parents' death several years later that pushed Victoria back to church. The experience during her time at college had made her utterly dependent upon them, especially as she had been out of work for long periods. She hadn't told her parents about what had happened with John and for years she disguised the experience behind a different version of events. She simply said that she had discovered John was having an affair with someone else, so she'd realised that the best thing to do was to distance herself from him. John and Victoria never met after that tragic night at his flat and Victoria never had another serious relationship. But when her parents died—they both died in old age within three months of each other—the minister who took the funeral suggested to Victoria that she might like to come to church.

One Sunday, she did, and the minister preached a sermon on the parable of the prodigal son. Victoria (and probably everyone else in church that Sunday) knew the story well, but the minister encouraged the congregation to take a different approach to the account in Luke's Gospel and to imagine what life was like for the prodigal son in the months after his return. Victoria went home and, over lunch, did as the minister had suggested—and she found that she travelled back into an amazingly imaginative world, where she envisaged how those first few months provided the runaway with a second chance. Now she realised that she wanted the same thing for herself. However, she recognised that before she could even begin thinking of a second chance, she had work to do on herself. She decided to visit Lough Derg as part of this process, which is where I met her.

At the time, I was a theology student at Trinity College Dublin, and my Lough Derg visit took place after Easter. We had observed Holy Week at the college chapel with due diligence and felt that it would be worthwhile to follow it up with a pilgrimage to Lough Derg. Getting there was not easy. We travelled by train to Donegal and then caught a taxi in order to be there by 10.30 in the morning, the appointed time for the beginning of each pilgrimage. In many ways, it was an odd place to go in any Easter period—a time of rejoicing and celebration in the light of Christ's glorious resurrection—but we did go and I still can't remember why! It was an odd choice because it is one of the most austere places of pilgrimage that I have ever encountered.

In Chapter 5, I mentioned that one of the main reasons for going on pilgrimage during the Middle Ages was to seek God's forgiveness through penitence and absolution. My experience in Lough Derg showed me that thousands of pilgrims every year still search for space to find forgiveness and unload sins. I found Lough Derg to be an amazing place: it was like stepping back 500 years and seeing pilgrims in their hundreds seeking God's mercy and forgiveness. Over time, I have been reminded again and again that this search for forgiveness, in order to have a second chance in life, is still very much part of today's pilgrimage experience. On almost every pilgrimage I lead or participate in, there is someone seeking either God's forgiveness or the forgiveness of some one else, or even forgiveness of themselves for hidden personal limitations.

A UNIQUE PILGRIMAGE ISLAND

Station Island—or, as it is sometimes called, St Patrick's Purgatory —survives today as a living remnant of the early Irish church's tenacity and witness, which spans some 15 centuries. It is a unique pilgrimage island located in a lake, Lough Derg, in County Donegal. Station Island is one of 46 small islands on the lake and it has been a place of serious penitential pilgrimage since the dawn of Irish Christianity. Its fame stemmed from a vision of purgatory—a passage into another world—which St Patrick is said to have had in a cave on one of the other islands in the lake.

There has been a Christian monastic settlement here since the fifth century. On the island where St Patrick himself is believed to have stayed a while (Saint's Island), he established a settlement of Christian monks, and tradition has it that the first abbot of this monastery was St Davog, a disciple of St Patrick. While there is very little historical evidence either proving or disproving these direct links with Patrick, there are references in two significant ancient manuscripts—the *Annals of Ulster* and the *Annals of the Four Masters*—to the existence of a monastery on the lake. In 1184, one of the resident monks records that a pilgrimage had taken place on the island and he states that, by staying on the island, pilgrims will gain substantial spiritual benefits. By the mid twelfth century, the Augustinian order had arrived in Ireland and established a monastery on the lake. From that point on, Lough Derg became one of Europe's major pilgrimage destinations, with hundreds of people seeking to catch a glimpse of the other world through St Patrick's cave. By this stage, the Irish church had become deeply integrated into the fabric of Roman Christendom, and this, along with the international prestige of the Augustinians, made communications to and from Ireland relatively easy. The Augustinians are noted for the way in which they preserved and promoted their shrines and holy places throughout Europe, and it is in this period that the main historical evidence for the penitential importance of pilgrimages to the islands of Lough Derg emerges.

AN EXPERIENCE MORE THAN A PLACE

From the moment I set foot on Station Island and realised the extent and depth of its penitential nature, there were two questions that I kept asking myself. What was it about this remarkable place that had not only preserved its history but also its continuing popularity, especially among young people? Why did Lough Derg continue to attract so many modern-day pilgrims? In an age when it is unpopular and considered somewhat old-fashioned to use words such as 'sin', 'absolution' and 'penance', it is hard to believe that the very essence of a Lough Derg pilgrimage could attract anyone. This is what makes it a place of both paradox and contradiction. It is paradoxical because, although people usually shy away from discussing sin in general, let alone their own sins, this is a place founded on the self-exposure of personal sin in order to have a second chance in life. Similarly, it is a place of contradiction because it goes against many of the accepted values of our contemporary world, by offering pilgrims the very opposite of what human beings yearn for most—glitter, comfort, pleasure and rest. This is not a place for the faint-hearted, but I discovered very early on that it is certainly a place for the serious pilgrim—the one who truly believes that the message of the gospel provides the key to understanding some of the greater intricacies of human existence.

One of the things that strikes me most about Lough Derg each time I visit is that, unlike many other pilgrimage destinations, it is not the place that makes the pilgrimage attractive but the experience. The place itself is difficult to reach; it is bleak and inhospitable and there are no stones or monuments through which to explore its history. Also, as a place, it stands somewhat apart from the other major pilgrim destinations of the world. It does not have the glamour of direct association with Christ himself that the sites of Palestine have, for instance. Nor has it ever been hallowed by the bones of great saints such as those of Peter and James that draw hordes of pilgrims to Rome or Compostela. It has never possessed the relics considered by medieval pilgrims as essential centrepieces for any successful pilgrimage shrine. Rather, its power has always been in both the experience that pilgrims seek on the island and the fulfilment they attain through immersing themselves in that experience. For many, as it is for me, the depth of Lough Derg is in the seeking and the attaining—a seeking after ways to unburden oneself so as to attain peace, in which a fresh start can be made and a second chance received.

BEGINNING THE PILGRIMAGE

My first visit to Lough Derg began with a long train journey from Dublin to Donegal. Three of us then caught a taxi to the lakeside, from which rowing boats took pilgrims across to the island where we were shown to the hostel in order to claim a cubicle. We were told to remove our shoes and socks because we had to remain barefoot for the whole of the three-day pilgrimage. We also ate only one meal a day—black tea or coffee, oatcakes and dry toast—as fasting is an important part of the pilgrimage on Lough Derg. There is a long tradition of fasting in the Christian Church. In the Old Testament, it is usually associated with sorrow for sin and a turning to God in times of distress (see Nehemiah 9:1; Esther 4:3; Jeremiah 36:6; Psalm 35:13). It was often accompanied by wailing, lamentation, walking barefoot and wearing sackcloth and ashes. The early Christians carried over many religious observances from their Jewish roots and fasting was one of the most important of these (Matthew 17:21; Mark 9:29; Acts 14:23; 1 Corinthians 7:5).

The first day of the pilgrimage was memorable: we were first required to meet as a group in St Patrick's Basilica to give thanks for our safe arrival. This was followed by a period of walking around barefoot, pausing at five specifically located prayer stations, all dedicated to Irish saints (Patrick, Brigid, Brendan, Catherine and

Columba), to pray and to open our hearts to God's presence. After the barefoot walk, we returned to the Basilica, where we remained in prayer all night—a discipline known as the Vigil. The Gospels tell us of various occasions when Jesus sought solitude in order to pray (Matthew 14:23; Mark 1:35; 6:46; Luke 5:16). Perhaps the prototype for the Lough Derg Vigil is to be found in the garden of Gethsemane, where Jesus spent the night in prayer (Mark 14:32–42). Christ's command to his disciples on that occasion to stay awake and to pray has drawn a response from devout Christians ever since.

It is on the second day at Lough Derg that the pilgrims get to the heart of the matter: on that day they renew baptismal vows, participate in the sacrament of reconciliation, confess sins and spend the day walking the various prayer stations and praying. It's only on the second night that they get to sleep in their hostel cubicle. On the third and final day, pilgrims celebrate the Eucharist, put their shoes back on and spend some time at the prayer stations reflecting on the pilgrimage and preparing for the fresh start that many come to Lough Derg to discover.

MEETING VICTORIA

It was as I made my way out of the Basilica on that final morning, following the celebration of the Eucharist, that I met Victoria. We found ourselves heading for the same prayer station, St Brigid's Cross. This is where all the pilgrimages on Lough Derg start on the first day and I was keen to do my final reflecting precisely where I had started exploring myself in this extraordinary place—and Victoria had the same idea in mind.

We arrived at the prayer station together and began to chat. It was the last morning for both of us and we talked about how extreme the pilgrimage had been but how, at the heart of the extremity, something profound had happened to us both. We compared our respective experiences and spoke about what had brought us there. In good Lough Derg tradition, we gave each other space to tell our respective stories. Victoria told me hers first, and said how a chance conversation with someone from Ireland who attended her church had given her the 'crazy idea' of travelling to Lough Derg. Now she was so pleased that she had done so.

One of the things that she repeated several times was the fact that the experience of Lough Derg had helped her realise that, for many years, she had been grieving deeply for the loss of the whole and happy person she might have been. She said that the all-night vigil on the previous day had given her the opportunity she so desperately needed to rediscover her blocked-out trauma and allow space for her painful memories to surface. For years, she had felt disturbed by unresolved issues about her identity and her sexual hang-ups. Her tragic experience with John had meant that she struggled almost every day with depression, loneliness and lack of self-esteem. Gone were her dreams of romance and tender love, of a white wedding and living happily ever after. Instead, Victoria's adult life had been filled with feelings of hurt and degradation because she had just not been able to find a way of escaping her past and moving on in her personal journey.

Sadly, stories of sexual abuse like Victoria's are all too common, and have been for generations. Such abuse attacks the physical, psychological and spiritual integrity of human beings. For many people, particularly women and children, it is not an exaggeration to suggest that it is more common for sex to be experienced as a commodity—an instrument of abuse and alienation and control— than as an expression of mutual enjoyment.

Kathy Galloway, a member of the Iona Community and at one time its leader, writes of how the sheer scale and extent of the abuse of sex creates a climate of vulnerability and fear, which shapes the daily experience and relationships of many people (*Dreaming of Eden*, Wild Goose Publications, 1997). She goes on to give stark examples of the consequences that resonate with so many of us: a woman afraid to go out at night, a man wary about showing affection to his daughter, a woman squirming in silent embarrassment at her colleague's offensive comments, an abused child too frightened to tell anybody what is happening. Such examples witness to horrible distortions at the very heart of everyday life. Victoria is only one among millions caught up in a web of abuse and transgression.

TRUE SELF-KNOWLEDGE

Too often, such personal stories remain on the periphery of theological pronouncements and church teaching, which are generally based on tradition, theory and long-established rules—deductively and theoretically derived rather than experientially well-informed. Too often, church teaching is forged in isolation from human experience, beginning with principles that are applied to people's lives and resulting in what the contemporary feminist theologian Elaine Graham describes as a dislocation between theological discourse and pastoral situations (*Spiritual Dimensions of Pastoral Care*, Jessica Kingsley, 2000).

Surely, an authentic interpretation of the Christian life has no room for such perfectionist ethics. Faith should be solidly based in the God-given reality of the world, where the events of people's real everyday lives matter deeply. My own experiences as a Christian pastor and pilgrimage leader have convinced me that there is not and never can be such a thing as a perfect human being which we are all called to become—but this is another paradox of the faith we share. The Christian life is centred on the person of Christ, not his rule book, and it is in Christ that we come to realise the fullness of God's unfolding revelation to us as individuals. Christ's call to each one of us is to be honestly and authentically ourselves.

I have found that within the shared experience of pilgrimage participants gradually but eventually come to an important point of self-awareness. They may well discover that the person they are growing into, due very often to the influence of others around them and their own reaction to such influence, is not as whole and harmonious as they might like. The dawning of this self-awareness offers the opportunity to embrace an ongoing process of personal healing. Accepting, as gift and as grace, the wounded people we discover ourselves to be, we can learn to live as fully as we can within our personal limitations. To do this is to be truly alive.

One of the most important pilgrimage lessons I have ever learnt is that it takes a lifetime to get to know ourselves fully. But, as we grow to recognise our true identities, we become only too well aware of our own need of healing and how this, too, is a lifelong process. It is only as we learn to live with our own honest stories that we discover hope for the ongoing journey. It also needs to be remembered that healed wounds continue to leave scars, but, in our remembering, grace and strength are revealed in and through those scars.

A Bible passage that I often reflect on with pilgrims is the account of Jacob wrestling with God at the river Jabbok (Genesis 32:22–32). It's an enigmatic story that speaks of a real physical struggle—a wrestling with God from which Jacob seems to emerge as the winner. During the struggle, Jacob recognises the supernatural character of his adversary and extorts a blessing from him. The text avoids using the name of God, however, and the unknown antagonist refuses to give his name. The wrestling lasts all night—as did our vigil in Lough Derg—and Jacob's hip is dislocated. As a result of the injury, he leaves the following morning with a limp, a kind of scar. I often wonder whether, from that moment on, his strength was actually in some way in that limp. Because he fought and struggled all night with God, by the morning he had come to realise something of his own limitations; as he moved on from that extraordinary encounter, he was not only scarred but the stronger for it. Just like Jacob, each of us can learn to bear the unique scars of our healed wounds and see that they enhance our individual humanity because they represent an integral part of what we have learnt about ourselves.

REPENTANCE AND HEALING

In his book on pilgrimage, Ian Bradley ends his section on Lough Derg with a quotation from one of the priests in the Basilica. That priest told the pilgrims that in Lough Derg there are no outsiders and that, because no one wore shoes, all were equal. He said that people journey together on pilgrimage and share their joy and pain, and that in Lough Derg not only are people's individual stories heard but help is offered as pilgrims leave to continue their life's journey.

As the time came for me to leave Lough Derg, that last conversation between Victoria and me taught both of us that the bearing of our woundedness and the recognition of the pain it brings into our lives is the very stuff out of which repentance and healing are born. At last, in this astonishingly severe place of penitential pilgrimage, Victoria recognised that to acknowledge her need for healing and forgiveness (as all human beings need healing and forgiveness, whether they are victims or aggressors) was an inescapable stage in the process of being healed and forgiven.

❊

—————— *Chapter 10* ——————

CANTERBURY: DEALING WITH DISAPPOINTMENTS

PETER AND JEAN

Peter and his wife Jean had been married for almost 30 years. Although they had always intended to have children, for all sorts of reasons they never actually got round to it. Both of them were hard workers: Peter worked for a trade union and Jean was a nurse. Originally, Peter had hoped to follow his father in the family carpentry business, but after his father's death he just couldn't keep the business going and had to sell it; the trade union job was a fallback.

Over a period of two years, Jean had been suffering from what she thought was a series of minor ailments and had had to take periods off work. One day, Peter came home from the office and found Jean sobbing because she had received some very bad news. The hospital had informed her that she was suffering from an inoperable ovarian cancer and in less than a week she would be starting a long regime of chemotherapy. Peter was devastated and that evening they both talked well into the early hours. What had they done to deserve what was happening? How could they possibly have sinned so much as to end up with a lot like this? It was clear that they had several major disappointments: no children, Peter's whole adult life in a job he had not really enjoyed, and now cancer.

Jean lived with cancer for almost 18 months. In many ways, the first few months were almost bearable, as she still had strength for a reasonable quality of life. There was hope and there were long conversations and some opportunities to do things that she and Peter had not done together for years. They talked a lot about their life together and about what they had done and what they had missed out on. A lot of the talk was about how short life is and how crucial it is to make the most of every moment. Jean kept saying that she'd thought she would live for ever.

Although Jean had been informed from the outset that her health would not improve and that her illness was terminal, she and Peter were determined to fight. From the start, they had a choice— palliative care with space to live together and enjoy what time they had left or, alternatively, chemotherapy to keep the cancer at bay for a while but with all the turbulence of that invasive treatment. They took the second option: Jean was rapidly sapped of her energy, and life became very difficult and uncomfortable.

The last twelve months of Jean's life were hell. Peter arranged for compassionate leave from work to care for her and their life was turned completely upside down. It was one hospital visit after another, followed by recurring secondary illnesses and side effects from the medication. Peter found the whole experience so hard that, when Jean eventually died, it took him months to rediscover any kind of balance to his life. His feelings of intense disappointment and personal inadequacy almost got the better of him. A family friend suggested that he would benefit from taking some time out of routine things. Maybe he should consider a holiday or, even better, a pilgrimage with a group of people. Peter agreed and began thinking of an appropriate place to go.

As a child, I had an aunt living in London and was fortunate to be able to visit her regularly during school holidays and enjoy wandering aimlessly around the city, getting to know its delights. On one occasion she took me to Canterbury Cathedral: I was fascinated and promised myself a return visit some time in the future. That promise was fulfilled over 20 years later, when I noticed an advert for a weekend pilgrimage to Canterbury in a church newspaper. It looked interesting because it followed the northern route to Canterbury, starting at St Edward the Confessor's church in Westminster, otherwise known as Westminster Abbey.

Much of the pilgrimage was by coach and for part of the journey I sat next to Peter.

CANTERBURY: THE CATHEDRAL OF AUGUSTINE AND BECKET

As far as the history of pilgrimage in Britain is concerned, Thomas Becket is probably one of the best-known saints. It was his martyrdom in 1170 that gave Canterbury its unique position in relation to the other cathedrals and minsters of the age. He was canonised (declared a saint) in 1173, and the fire of the following year gave the monks of Canterbury a perfect opportunity to rebuild the cathedral and construct a magnificent setting for a shrine to house the remains of Thomas Becket—St Thomas of Canterbury. His fame spread throughout Europe with amazing speed and, soon after his death, Canterbury became a major place of pilgrimage.

However, Becket was not the first major saint to be associated with Canterbury, by any stretch of the imagination. As far back as the sixth century, Pope Gregory the Great was concerned about the state of the Christian faith in Britain. Although Christianity had reached Britain some time late in the third century, the departure of the Romans as an occupying force changed the British way of life dramatically. In that aftermath period, British rulers such as Vortigern encouraged the tribes of northern Europe—the Angles, the Saxons and the Jutes—to help protect British territory from the invading Picts from the north. These northern European mercenaries rapidly became just another occupying force and brought with them an unremittingly pagan culture. Consequently, the

117

Christian faith was pushed to the west—Cornwall, the south-west of Scotland, some western parts of England and the high mountain ranges of Wales.

In 597 (the year that Columba died on Iona), Pope Gregory sent Augustine to convert these pagan tribes and re-establish the Christian faith in the eastern parts of Britain. It would be a great mistake, however, to think of this as the date when Christianity reached Britain. A great deal of historical evidence is available to show that the Christian faith flourished in Britain long before Augustine reached Canterbury. Even some of the Church Fathers of the very early Christian centuries—Tertullian, Origen, Justin Martyr, Hilary of Poitiers and Athanasius—refer to Britain in relation to Christianity.

In Britain itself, some key figures were emerging within the church, who were proving themselves competent theologians and were seeking to preserve in their writings the traditions that had reached Britain during and soon after the Roman occupation. In around 480, Constantius wrote about Germanus of Auxerre's visit to Britain to help Christians in their battles against the followers of Pelagius. Another British bishop, Finian, who taught Columba of Iona, wrote a major document on penance and sin in about 550 and shows in his writings the close connections between the British and Irish churches. The Welsh monk Gildas, writing in about 540, offers a critique of the British church in the post-Roman period, while Patrick's letters and the writings of others, such as Samson, Illtyd and Pelagius, all prove the existence of astute theological reflection in Britain at this time. Then there is the important historical reference to three British bishops attending the Council of Arles in 314: the bishops of London, York and Colchester, along with other priests and deacons.

Clearly, Pope Gregory was no fool and he would have known about this early Christian presence in Britain. His main concern was probably to maintain the Christian tradition in the east of Britain, where the pagan tribes of northern Europe had had most impact.

With this overriding aim in mind, he sent the monk Augustine from his own former monastery of St Andrew in Rome to the south-eastern shores of Britain in 597. Eventually Augustine was able to establish Canterbury as his missionary base and his work among the people brought the pagan traditions of the Angles, the Saxons and the Jutes directly in touch with the old, Greco-Roman Christianity of the Mediterranean. The Anglo-Saxon church was about to take its place among the provinces of the Roman Western world.

CHURCH AND KING

Augustine and his companions landed in Thanet and almost immediately made contact with Aethelberht, the king of Kent. The writings of Bede tell us that this king was one of the most powerful British leaders at the time. Although Aethelberht was not a Christian, he had married a Christian wife, Bertha. She was a Frankish princess who had, interestingly, been allowed by her husband to bring with her Liuthard, the Bishop of Senlis, as her private chaplain, and together they were allowed to practise their faith. Their worship was centred at St Martin's Church in Canterbury, and Bede informs us that it is quite possible that this church was originally built while the Romans were still in Britain. However, on receiving these Mediterranean Christians, Aethelberht decided to give them permission to base their missionary work in Canterbury, already the seat of his government. In the course of time, the king was converted and Augustine was consecrated the Archbishop of the English. Work began on building churches in various places and it was not long before a cathedral was erected in Canterbury, dedicated to the Holy Saviour and St Augustine.

For the purposes of this book, we can now jump almost 500 years to the story of Thomas Becket, the son of an immigrant Norman merchant living in London. Although Becket originally trained as a knight, he eventually entered the household of Theobald, the then Archbishop of Canterbury. He studied on the Continent and worked for a while in Rome before being ordained a priest. After a spell as the Archdeacon of Canterbury, Becket was made King Henry II's Chancellor; then, in 1162, he became Archbishop of Canterbury.

Becket and Henry were close friends until a feud over issues surrounding the rights of the clergy developed between them. Eventually the feud became a major part of a serious power struggle between church and state in England, which subsequently developed into a conflict between the British church and Rome. While Becket was on the Continent, Henry II arranged for the coronation of his son as co-regent. The ceremony was performed in the absence of Becket by the Archbishop of York and the Bishops of London and Salisbury. Becket was furious because he believed that coronations should be performed only by the Archbishop of Canterbury. He arranged for the bishops involved to be punished and they in turn appealed to the king. It was at this stage that Henry impetuously voiced a wish to be rid of 'this turbulent priest'. On 29 December 1170, Becket was murdered in Canterbury Cathedral by four of the king's knights. His martyrdom forced confessions from the king and he was canonised just three years later. The following year, King Henry did penance at his tomb.

CANTERBURY PILGRIMS

Within days of Becket's martyrdom, pilgrims began to converge on the cathedral amid reports that people were being cured at his tomb, and the reputation of Canterbury as a centre of pilgrimage spread rapidly. Probably the most vivid glimpse of such pilgrims is preserved in Geoffrey Chaucer's *Canterbury Tales*, written in the 14th century. In 1338, at the age of 48, Chaucer himself went to Canterbury as a pilgrim. It may well have been on this occasion that he had the brilliant idea of collecting tales from among a party of 29 pilgrims—tales recounted to occupy pilgrims on a long journey and to help them enjoy one another's company.

Over the years, pilgrimages to Canterbury have contributed immensely to the prosperity of the city, and 'The Pilgrims' Way' became the most famous of all of England's pilgrimage routes. There are still two well-travelled routes on offer to Canterbury pilgrims—a northern route and a southern one. While the northern route begins in London, the southern route begins in Winchester, one of the great ancient cities of England, where the pilgrims traditionally gathered at St Swithin's church in the city centre: Swithin was bishop of Winchester in 852. I have described the two routes in detail elsewhere (*Every Pilgrim's Guide to Celtic Britain and Ireland*, Canterbury Press, 2002). As with other places of pilgrimage that offer more than one route to the destination, it is common for the routes—however many of them—to have a place of convergence where all the pilgrims come together. The two routes to Canterbury meet at the village of Aylesford, just over 30 miles from the city.

As we have already seen, just as in centuries past, so people today opt to become pilgrims for all sorts of reasons. Indeed, one of the things I enjoy most about leading pilgrimages is the chance to have conversations along the way about what has motivated individuals to join. I had two reasons for becoming a Canterbury pilgrim on the occasion when I met Peter. The first was to fulfil the promise I had made to myself many years ago while visiting Canterbury with my aunt; the second was a slightly more immediate reason. That year, I had a particularly heavy load of pilgrimages to lead. I was due to lead five large groups of Americans and Canadians to Ynys Enlli, as well as a pilgrimage from my own parish to Iona and another group of pilgrims from across Wales to Santiago de Compostela. To be spiritually nourished for these adventures, I felt the need to become a pilgrim myself for a while, so I applied for a place on the Canterbury pilgrimage and headed for the gathering place in Westminster late one Friday afternoon.

AN ENCOUNTER ALONG THE WAY

At Westminster Abbey, we paused for a while at the Shrine of St Edward the Confessor, who reigned over England from 1042 to 1066. Before St George was adopted as the patron saint of England in the 14th century, it was Edward who held this illustrious position. Two things made an impact on me as we came to Edward's shrine.

First, here was the shrine of a man who had ruled at a time of turbulence and on the threshold of great changes. During his reign there were serious struggles between France and England, and the arrival of the Normans in 1066 changed the face of British Christianity. However, in these struggles Edward's diplomacy meant that he became an important symbol of reconciliation between the French and the English. For many of us in the group, that was a useful opening for our pilgrimage—and the words 'turbulence', 'threshold' and 'reconciliation' remained with me throughout. Turbulence in life is a common reason for seeking opportunities for pilgrimage today. Often while on pilgrimage, a threshold emerges, leading to new opportunities, and the return home becomes an experience of reconciliation.

Second, Edward was the last crowned Saxon king of England. I felt that, as such, he brought to an end a significant era, which had started with the conversion of Aethelberht through the ministry of Augustine. At his shrine I reflected that 1066 brought British Christians to a kind of full circle: the year 597 marked the arrival of one significant group of people from the Continent and 1066 marked the arrival of another. Pilgrimage is often a 'circular' kind of experience, where we find that travelling to a distant place helps us to discover the value of what we had before—which is often staring us in the face!

The following day of the pilgrimage was one of travel along the whole of the northern route, aiming to arrive in Canterbury early in the evening so that Sunday could be spent entirely in and around the cathedral. The route would take us through Greenwich, Dartford, Gravesend, Rochester, Aylesford, Maidstone and Harbledown, stopping along the way at significant places. It was over lunch in Rochester that I first met Peter, and he became my travelling companion on the coach the rest of the way to Canterbury. If my main motive for becoming a Canterbury pilgrim had been to seek spiritual nourishment to strengthen me for the pilgrimages I would lead in the coming months, Peter's reasons were very different. It was several months before this pilgrimage that his wife, Jean, had died and he was still grieving deeply. We chatted along the way and shared different stories about ourselves and our hopes for the pilgrimage.

Our stop in Rochester made me think again of Augustine's arrival in Canterbury 1400 years ago. Two of his Roman companions on that crucial mission, Paulinus and Justus, are remembered here, as they were both buried in Rochester; indeed, it was Justus who founded the cathedral in 604. But Rochester also has another, in many ways less well-known shrine, that of St William. In 1201, William, a young Scottish man, was on his way from Scotland to Jerusalem and wanted to travel by way of Canterbury. Sadly, he never made it further than Rochester, for he was murdered there, only to be raised through the miraculous actions of a woman who discovered his dead body and covered it with honeysuckle, with the result that he came back to life. Today, a hospital named after William stands near the spot where this miracle took place. Peter told me later, on the coach, that as our pilgrimage leader was telling this story, his mind went back to Jean and to his intense disappointment that, unlike William, she had not been cured. It's always interesting to see how different pilgrimage places affect people in different ways, and it is only in the retelling and sharing of stories along the way that sense is made of the significance of a place for different people. The shrine of Edward the Confessor made the strongest impression on me, while, for Peter, it was the memory of William, the young Scottish man whose pilgrim journey ended at Rochester.

PAIN, SICKNESS AND SUFFERING

Issues surrounding pain, sickness and suffering have always been foremost on the list of reasons why Christians participate in the ancient practice of pilgrimage: certainly these were some of the issues that brought Peter to Canterbury. Questions regarding pain, sickness and suffering haunt many of us, and, despite the sting of such questions, facing them is fundamental to what it means to be human. But not everyone experiences pain, sickness and suffering in quite the same way or with equal intensity or for an equal length of time. Similarly, not everyone responds to such difficulties in the same way. For some, they are, strangely enough, the making of their character, but for others, such as for Peter and Jean, they spell destruction. Some reach for the bottle of pills—or some other bottle—while some turn to prayer, and, in order to try to make some sense of his own story, Peter eventually turned to being a Canterbury pilgrim.

When Christians think about pain, sickness and suffering, we find that pain is often interpreted in terms to do with punishment and penalty; sickness as being spiritually or morally ailing, corrupted through sin or wrongdoing; suffering as to have something (painful, distressing or injurious) inflicted upon us. These definitions suggest something crucial about what suffering people have to bear, whether or not they are physically sick or in pain—that their circumstances are something imposed on them, something others may find distasteful and may even blame them for, something they may blame themselves for.

Throughout my conversations with Peter about his suffering and his sense of lifelong disappointment, I became more and more convinced that as we experience pain, sickness, blame, guilt, powerlessness and disappointment—whether our own or other people's—what is of central importance is achieving a sense of meaning. This is not so much at the level of 'making sense' of what is happening, of asking what the meaning is of this or that event. Rather, it's about arriving at a place in life—in the middle of our experience of suffering, where our sweat and blood are being poured out and our fight with circumstances is at its fiercest—and recognising, even accepting, that only one act remains: to search for the well of God-given strength deep within our hearts and thereby discover, through the pain, a power we did not know we had. Only then can we begin to reach for any sense of 'meaning'. The individual sufferer is never powerless but that power is not always apparent even to themselves. The true measure of this power is not about how others perceive it but about how it helps the suffering person to endure their own situation.

This is the power that Jesus found on the mount of transfiguration as he recognised the difficulties that lay ahead for him (Matthew 17:1–13), and in Gethsemane shortly before his arrest (Mark 14:32–42). In the same way, perhaps, this is the power that the prodigal son discovered when he realised the time had come to return home, seek his father's forgiveness and face up to his brother's dismay (Luke 15:11–32). After the resurrection of Jesus, reflecting on their encounter with the risen Lord, this is the power that the two disciples from Emmaus discovered as they walked together and found the strength to return to the others and proclaim the hope they had found (Luke 24:13–35). By going to a place apart—which may or may not be an 'official' place of pilgrimage—Christians have constantly found the strength required to continue, even though their life circumstances remain as challenging as before.

ARRIVING AT THE DESTINATION—AND THE RETURN HOME

We arrived at Canterbury early on Saturday evening, and on Sunday our short pilgrimage ended with a celebration of the Eucharist in the cathedral. After enjoying a coffee at the end of the service, Peter suggested that he and I retire to a corner of the cathedral for some final reflections. As this was his first pilgrimage ever, he felt the need to talk over a few of the things he had experienced, both within and around him. We headed towards Trinity Chapel, probably the ultimate goal of every Canterbury pilgrim who wishes to visit the shrine of St Thomas Becket. It was in 1220, after the rebuilding of the cathedral, that Becket's relics were carried in a chest and placed in a shrine in the Trinity Chapel, in the presence of King Henry III. Leading up to the chapel are some steps—the Pilgrim Steps—and it is easy to see how the hollows in these ancient steps have been worn by the tread of innumerable pilgrims over many generations. Now our footsteps contributed to those hollows. It seemed appropriate to sit on the steps and have our reflection there.

It was appropriate for another reason, too. At the beginning of the pilgrimage, Peter and I had been encouraged to reflect on our personal circumstances at a deeper level as we paused to remember two other people connected to the Canterbury pilgrimage. For me it had been Edward the Confessor, and for Peter it had been the young Scottish pilgrim, St William. The three words associated with Edward—turbulence, threshold and reconciliation—had remained with me throughout the pilgrimage. Now Peter and I both agreed that the Canterbury journey had offered us a threshold from which we could move onwards to reconcile our own personal and different sense of turbulence. In a similar way, Peter had found his encounter at the memorial to William a kind of threshold moment. William never made it to Canterbury, let alone to Jerusalem, but 800 years later here we were, two 21st-century pilgrims, still talking about him. Peter found comfort in this, not least because he was now certain that Jean's spirit would somehow endure. The journey had shown him that she would never be forgotten because he would always remember her, and that, after years of marriage, she was now in some way part of him although no longer physically present.

My wish of many years before had been fulfilled and I had been sufficiently refreshed and nourished to face the pilgrimage load that awaited me back home. As for Peter, he found the whole experience a homecoming from a personal exile that had lasted for many years. It was not a matter of saying that the pilgrimage helped him to get over Jean's death—not at all. Rather, he found in the experience of the Pilgrim's Way to Canterbury a rich source of inspiration which helped him discover a power that would eventually, he believed, lead him on to a balanced, joyful and peaceful way of being. He stopped talking endlessly about disappointments and began thinking of his sufferings as opportunities through which to look at life—the whole of life—as a pilgrimage towards the eternal.

✻

Chapter 11

IONA: STRIVING FOR UNITY

DYLAN

Dylan had been the Anglican priest of his parish for almost a year. It was an interesting area, not geographically large but one that contained four reasonably strong Christian denominations: Anglican, Methodist, Presbyterian and Congregationalist. Dylan was the only ordained minister in the parish, as none of the other congregations had managed to afford a minister for a number of years. Following his induction as the rector of the parish, one of the first things Dylan did was to visit the deacons and officers of the other three churches. This made a lasting impression on those people and word got around that Dylan was a devoted and enthusiastic ecumenist.

Dylan had been brought up in a mixed denominational family: his father was a Methodist and his mother a Roman Catholic, but, as there was no local Catholic church, his parents opted to associate him with the Anglican Sunday school. Subsequently, when Dylan went to university, he chose to worship at the Anglican chaplaincy and found himself well and truly rooted in the Anglican tradition. But he was convinced that the authentically Christian Church was one that looked for every chance to create links and participate in activities that involved all Christians—not just the ones that 'did the same thing as us'.

When Dylan trained for ordination, he was keen to establish himself as an ecumenist. Obviously he was Anglican but he took every opportunity to study and practise ecumenism. He had never really thought of becoming a non-conformist minister or a Catholic priest but he was absolutely convinced that, one day, these distinctions would be less important. Dylan longed for the day when he could serve as a priest in a community where church divisions meant very little and where Christians of all denominations worshipped together. A key scripture passage for him was Jesus' prayer in the upper room, in which he asked his Father that all his followers might be one (John 17:21–23). Dylan was particularly attracted to this text because it was one of the last truths that Jesus shared with his friends before his arrest and subsequent death.

As Dylan's first year in that ministry passed by, the people of the parish grew to recognise his determination to work closely with all the Christians of the area, regardless of their denomination. The Presbyterians, Methodists and Congregationalists warmed to his approach and arranged for Dylan to conduct services on a monthly basis in their respective churches. Each time he was responsible for leading worship in one of the 'other' churches, all three denominations united and offered Dylan tremendous support. One Monday evening, the Anglicans were holding their Parochial Church Council and Dylan planned to talk enthusiastically about his ecumenical vision in the hope of bringing them on board. He was passionate about the importance of Christian people working together at every level and at every opportunity. He intended to discuss the future of joint services, as well as other ecumenical ventures and a parish mission that would involve all the churches. His primary intention was to talk about the Christian community, regardless of denomination, as a pilgrim church, travelling together in that particular place.

As the meeting got underway, Dylan began by outlining his plan and saying that he looked forward to a positive and fruitful discussion. He was about to be disappointed. The meeting re-mained silent for a few minutes until one of the churchwardens asked who was paying his stipend and whether the 'others' were planning to make a financial contribution. Another parishioner asked whether Dylan was planning to visit the Anglican families before he knocked on the doors of other Christians. Someone else wondered whether the bishop knew about these 'novel' ideas, and one even dared to ask whether Methodist baptisms would take precedence over Anglican ones. Dylan was taken aback and depressed by the response: he had never expected such negative and entrenched reactions. Some time later, the chance came for him to take a break and he decided to pay a visit to Iona, to see if the special atmosphere there of spiritual connection and reconciliation could re-energise his vision for ecumenical ministry.

VISITING IONA

A few years ago, I had the privilege of being invited to lead a retreat for a group of young people at the George MacLeod Centre on Iona. It was not my first visit to the island, as I had been twice before as a pilgrim, and I have been again since, but that particular visit proved to be by far the most significant. For me, a trip to Iona is not simple! It means a car journey to Bangor, then a train to Glasgow with two changes, another train to Oban, an overnight stay there and a ferry across to Mull, then a bus across Mull and a final brief ferry trip on to Iona followed by a short walk to the Abbey. This was the first time that I'd ventured the journey this way, as on previous occasions I had travelled to Oban by car. The problem this time was that I didn't know that I had to change railway stations in Glasgow and, assuming that I had plenty of time to get from one platform to another, I indulged in a cup of coffee. In some ways I wish I hadn't bothered: it meant I missed my connection to Oban and had to sleep on the platform to catch an early train the following morning. In other ways I'm glad I did, because it was on that early morning connecting train to Oban that I met Dylan. We sat next to each other during the journey and spent time together exploring Iona: he was excellent company.

COLUMBA SEARCHES FOR AN ISLAND

In his biography of Columba (the founder of the Celtic monastic community on Iona), Adamnan, the eighth abbot of Iona, writing between 688 and 692, informs us that Columba first landed on the island in May 563. He had sailed from Ireland at the age of 42 with twelve other companions, and remained there for 34 years. Interestingly, he died in 597, the very year that Augustine arrived in Canterbury. Columba was born in Donegal and, as well as establishing the monastic community on Iona, was also responsible for founding monasteries at Derry, Durrow and Kells. Although from a royal family, he decided at an early age to become a monk, studying under St Finian of Moville and St Finian of Clonard and being ordained priest by St Mobhi in Dublin.

It was traditional for Irish missionaries to settle on islands, as the sea offered them protection from enemies and an island could also offer a special kind of solitude in order to pursue a dual life of prayer and work. The story of Columba's first journey to Iona is an interesting one. Tradition states that St Molaise, one of his early spiritual directors, told him to seek an island from which Ireland could not be seen. Columba's group first touched land at Kintyre, then headed for the islands of the Inner Hebrides, but Ireland was still in sight. Eventually, as their coracle turned towards the Torren Rocks and Mull and Iona could be seen, they realised they had reached their destination.

Once on the island, Columba climbed one of the Iona hills, looked towards the north-west and still could not see Ireland. To this day, the hill is called Cairn-cul-ri-Erin, which means 'Cairn-of-back-to-Ireland'. Another interesting tradition states that when the monks landed on the island, they drew their coracle over a beach and on to a grassy slope, where they dug a hole and buried it. Again, to this day, a mound can be seen near the bay that is called Port-a-'Churaich, Port-of-the-Coracle, or simply St Columba's Bay. They then crossed inland, over what is still called the Machair, a flat and exposed area that led them to the foot of Dun I, the highest hill of Iona, where they found shelter and pasturage. This is where Columba built his first monastery, made of wood.

This original small group of monks probably erected several wooden huts and surrounded them with a rampart (known as a vellum) made of soil and stones for protection. Inside this protective enclosure would have stood a small church, a dormitory, a place for communal eating, an abbot's cell, a guesthouse and a kitchen. Gradually, the early monks would probably have attracted others to join them—not necessarily monks—and a supporting community developed outside the enclosure wall. Here, small and very basic barns, stables, work sheds and a mill would have been built, as well as a burial place, and here the so-called extended family would live, work and support the religious community.

THE SCRIPTORIUM

One of the early traditions associated with this and other Celtic (particularly Irish) monastic communities was the work of copying the scriptures for use in worship and spiritual direction. The actual writing and the materials used for the writing would have been housed in a scriptorium. The monastic scribes were noted for their skill in illuminating their copies of the scriptures with patterns and colourful depictions of biblical stories. They would have used goose and crow quills to copy the Gospels and the Psalms on parchment and wax tablets.

At the time of these early Celtic monks, the sea did not divide countries and continents but, rather, connected them. It was the monks' transport highway and their most direct means of communication, and it is clear that, from the very beginning of its Christian fame, Iona was constantly in touch with other Christian communities and played an influential role in the subsequent development of Western Christianity. In recent years there has been a great deal of research into the literary sources available to the early Christian community on Iona—the nature, quality and quantity of their books, manuscripts and Bibles. From the early manuscripts that emerged from this small island, it is clear that other writings were used and were thus responsible for shaping the Christian and monastic culture of both Iona and the areas of Britain influenced by Iona.

From the evidence of what happened in the scriptorium, the monks of Iona clearly had a deep devotion to the Bible. It was probably here that the creation of the highly decorated Book of Kells began, for instance. This Gospel book is one of seven surviving early Celtic biblical manuscripts written between the sixth and the ninth centuries—the others being the Books of Durrow, Armagh, Dimma and Mulling, and the Codex Usserianus I and Usserianus II—all forming a famous manuscript family currently housed at Trinity College, Dublin. What is striking is the sense of discipline and reverence that marks the pages of each one of these books, and the way in which they are part of a great tradition of fine writing and dedicated copying. The Book of Kells is probably the most famous of these manuscripts. It contains the Latin text of the four Gospels and is decorated by magnificent and intricate illuminated pages. The precise origins of the manuscript remain unclear but it is generally believed that it was started around the year 800 in the scriptorium on Iona.

Apart from the biblical material, the early Iona library also contained the biographies of various saints, such as Athanasius' *Life of Anthony*, Sulpicius Severus' *Life of Martin* and Constantius' *Life of Germanus of Auxerre*. There were also copies of Jerome's biblical commentaries, the writings of St Augustine of Hippo, Cassiodorus' *Exposition of the Psalms*, the *Dialogues* of Pope Gregory the Great, as well as various collections of poems and liturgical writings from both the Latin and Greek Fathers and more local Celtic writers such as Cogitosus, Cummene and Columba.

THE LEGACY OF THE IONA CHURCH

Clearly, then, Iona became an important place of study and a centre for the training of young monks and priests. The Rule of St Columba emphasised that the study and training should include three daily disciplines. He stressed that those in the Iona monastery should read the scriptures and other theological writings as often as possible, pray regularly (alone and with others) and not shun manual work. In his work on the Iona church, Ian Bradley attempts to identify what kind of church Iona sought to be and highlights three characteristics that appear to have been crucial. First, it was a church that had a firm devotional base built on regular prayer and the reading of scripture, especially the Psalms, as well as the study of religious poetry. Second, much of the literary activity of this church centred on a theology of praise in which God was celebrated as one who protected his people and revealed his presence in various ways. Third, it was a church that stressed the vitality of penance and the regular pattern of two-way pilgrimage—welcoming pilgrims into their midst and sending Iona monks out from the island to proclaim the gospel. Indeed, early Iona pilgrims made a vital contribution to the life of the churches in the north of Britain between the sixth and ninth centuries.

Although the sea provided access and good communications during Columba's lifetime, by the ninth century it had brought danger all along the British and Irish coasts. During the closing years of the eighth century, Viking raiders attacked Iona and killed many monks. Although life on the island was seriously affected, Iona was never abandoned, but it was not until the 13th century that the monastic life was completely restored and renewed. The

Benedictine Order established both a monastery and a nunnery on the island at this time and it is the remains of buildings from this period that can be seen today.

IONA'S INNER PILGRIMAGE

These ruined buildings, the fine examples of medieval crosses and several important natural features, such as the hill, the bays and the quarry, form the heart of an Iona pilgrimage today. Although the journey to the island is a pilgrimage in itself, once on Iona, people are invited to participate in a kind of inner pilgrimage using a number of contemporary themes. For the benefit of pilgrims, each day offers a different focus: Sunday's focus is on welcome, Monday's on justice and peace, Tuesday's on healing, Wednesday's on pilgrimage, Thursday's on commitment, Friday's on celebration and Saturday's on mission. Each of the seven themes is carefully woven into the devotional and liturgical life that is centred on the regular daily worship in the Abbey, as well as at the various prayer stations around the island.

From my experience, I would say that Wednesday is probably the most exciting day on Iona, when both the theme of the Abbey worship and the thrust of the various activities on the island is pilgrimage—a theme that brings together all that Iona seeks to achieve today. On Wednesdays from March to October, the community organises a pilgrimage walk around the whole island and everyone is invited to join in. The aim of the walk is to encourage pilgrims to use the prayer stations in order to reflect upon their own journeys of life. At each place there is a guided reflection, a time of silence and some prayers.

It was during one of these Wednesday pilgrimages that I was able to share fully in the predicament that confronted Dylan. It was a member of the Iona Community who had originally suggested to him that a visit to the island—and particularly the Wednesday walk—could be helpful for him. The walk began, as it always does, at the 1000-year-old St Martin's Cross. This is one of five ancient crosses on Iona but is the only one that is complete and still standing on its original site. It is probably close to Columba's original place of burial and, quite possibly, the site of the earliest church. What is striking about this cross is the number of different biblical stories depicted on it. On its west face, in the middle, the Blessed Virgin Mary with the baby Jesus can be seen, and carved down the shaft of the cross are Old Testament scenes such as Daniel in the lions' den and David playing the harp.

The pilgrims then pass what is known as St Columba's Cell, various monastery buildings and the Abbey—St Mary's Cathedral. One of the most impressive features of the abbey is the cloister, and at the centre of the cloister is a fine sculpture by Jacob Lipschitz, called 'The Descent of the Spirit'. On it is inscribed that, as a faithful Jew, Lipschitz hopes for goodwill among all people. It was here that Dylan began reflecting seriously on the issues of jealousy and entrenchment that confronted him back home. At this point on the pilgrimage walk, Iona shows less concern about relationship between Christians and more about the unity and integrity of all God's children—Jewish, Christian, Muslim and so forth.

The pilgrimage moves from the Abbey towards the remains of the nunnery, where pilgrims today are reminded of the balance that existed in the Celtic church between the feminine and the masculine—not just equality between men and women but, rather, the essential balance, the unity, between both. Walking through the village, pilgrims then pass Martyrs Bay, where, in 806, marauding Vikings slaughtered many monks. The memory of this act of terrible violence reminded us of all victims of torture and massacre in the contemporary world and the continuing task of healing and reconciliation that faces each one of us in different ways. As pilgrims approach the Machair, past the Hill of the Angels, where Columba is reputed to have been inspired by a vision of a heavenly host of angels, they see a large area of common grazing land, where the ancient monks tended their flocks and the later Benedictines grew corn. This is a place of great natural beauty and peace—a place shared by the natural world, animals and people. It seems that, at every stage of the pilgrimage, the message is for the whole of creation to be united, but for that to happen we must ourselves be united. We must be at peace with ourselves and in our home communities and recognise that the task of achieving unity among God's people starts with us.

A TURNING POINT FOR DYLAN

The Machair is traditionally the place where pilgrims pause for a shared picnic and afterwards walk towards St Columba's Bay by way of Loch Staonaig, the rocky pool, and the Marble Quarry. St Columba's Bay is a pebbled beach at the southern tip of Iona, where Columba is said to have first landed. As part of the meditation at the bay, pilgrims are asked to take two pebbles from the beach. One is thrown into the sea as a symbol of something in their lives they would like to leave behind, while the other they take back with them as a sign of a new commitment. This was a turning point for Dylan and he decided to leave behind his fear of searching for unity in the midst of aggressive detractors. The second pebble, he said, was his own strong commitment to those who supported him and longed to see the fulfilment of Christ's final prayer, that his people should be one.

This is often a significant stage in the pilgrimage for many pilgrims, and it is also the point where the walk back to the abbey begins, passing the Hermit's Cell—a spot where countless pilgrims have gone to seek solitude and silence to pray privately, and a place where they can experience something of the mystery of God. The more agile pilgrims are invited to climb Dun I immediately after pausing at the cell. Dylan and I did climb and we both felt a strong sense of achievement as we reached the stone cairn at the summit—achievement not because we had climbed to the top but because of what the pilgrimage had revealed to us. Throughout the Bible, mountains and hills are understood as places of vision and transfiguration, and this day on Iona had certainly helped us both to achieve a clearer vision of the way ahead and to glimpse the possibility of contemporary transfiguration.

Just two more pilgrimage stations remain: the Reilig Odhrain and St Oran's Chapel. The Reilig Odhrain, or Oran's Grave, is part of the ancient cemetery. Odhrain was Columba's cousin and the first of the original group that came with Columba to die and be buried on the island. St Oran's Chapel concludes the day's journey. It is the oldest of Iona's buildings, dating back to the twelfth century. A cemetery and a decayed building might seem to be odd places to end a pilgrimage, but was it not at a grave—an empty tomb— that the Christian story took an unexpected turn and provided a despairing group of followers with a new and astonishing hope? Paradoxically, resurrection and a sense of new beginning are often what we find in places of decay, death and hopelessness. At the end of our pilgrimage, Dylan and I were quite certain that our walk in the footsteps of Oran, Columba, the women of the island and the many people of faith who had made this journey before us would continue to inspire us and give us strength and vision for our own journeys of faith.

BUILDING UP COMMUNITY

The Iona Community today is an ecumenical group of men and women seeking new ways of living the gospel in the world. It was founded in 1938 by George MacLeod, at that time a parish minister in Glasgow, who was concerned by the church's blatant disengagement with local communities during a period of high unemployment and economic depression. He encouraged a regular flow of young Christians to Iona and began to rebuild the ruined abbey as a sign of hope in dark times. MacLeod was also keen to provide tangible evidence of the necessary integration of work, service, prayer and politics, and as such gave new birth to what both the Columban church and the Benedictine Order had done centuries before.

The modern-day Iona Community continues in this tradition and recognises as its primary work the task of building up community in a world marked by division, injustice and isolation. It is made up of well over 3000 people, including full members, associates and friends, drawn from a range of denominations and working backgrounds. Of course they do not all live on the island! The community is primarily a dispersed one, with members living all over Britain and beyond, and sharing a common discipline of a fivefold rule of daily prayer and Bible study, economic sharing, a proper use of time, meeting regularly as regional groups and working tirelessly for peace, reconciliation and justice.

Members of the Community who are resident on the island exercise a vital ministry of welcome to the thousands of pilgrims who come each year. The visitors are attracted to Iona for a wide range of reasons but, for me, three stand out. Firstly, the importance of Iona in the early history of Western Christianity continues to fascinate and draw people. As we have seen, after the arrival of Columba, Iona became one of the leading centres of Christian mission and learning in Europe. It was monks from Iona who went out to evangelise the people of Argyll, the Picts of northern Scotland and the Britons of north-east England. Iona missionaries also travelled as far as Germany and Russia to share the gospel. Their missionary activity had a dynamic, robust spirituality, which combined a profound mysticism with an abiding sense of the goodness and beauty of creation.

Secondly, pilgrims come searching for hope. The community continues to grow today as it recognises that there is an important and unfinished task facing Christians—namely, acknowledging that restoration is a sign of hope both for the church and for the world. Originally, the people whom George MacLeod attracted—craftsmen, trainee ministers and volunteers—came to restore an ancient abbey; today, pilgrims come to Iona to restore their own sense of perspective and be renewed in the calling to work for peace, reconciliation and justice.

Thirdly, pilgrims have always come simply to absorb the spirit of Iona itself and to participate in what has drawn like-minded people for generations. George MacLeod captured the spirit of Iona in his description of the island as a 'thin place'—the term that has become a universal description of places where pilgrims feel that heaven and earth are particularly close together.

PURSUING PEACE

One of the most distinctive features of the Iona Community, both on the island and throughout the world, is its unique worship pattern. As a community, the members affirm the centrality of worship and state that they owe their very existence to the gospel conviction that, in worship, we either give everything to God or we give nothing. On Iona, worship forms the backbone of all that is done; each day begins with communal prayer. I have always found it striking that, at the end of the morning service, no one kneels, as they do in many churches, to say a final quiet prayer. Rather, immediately after the closing words, the congregation remain standing and then leave with determination, going directly from worship into the heart of daily life to continue that same worship in different ways. The closing words of the service are a powerful testimony of this spiritual intent: 'We will not offer to God offerings that cost us nothing... we will seek peace and pursue it.'

In the evening the people meet again for prayer, but worship has been happening throughout the day in all that they have been doing. Also, it is at the close of the evening service alone that a blessing is given, and this is a blessing not simply to close an act of worship but to close a whole day of service to one another and to the risen Christ. For the Iona Community, the activities of the whole day are connected: work, worship and play are all part of one big liturgy, one work of service offered to God.

Our week on Iona was about to come to an end and, after the final night's farewell service, Dylan, three other friends and I decided to spend some time sitting around St Martin's Cross in order to reflect on the time we had spent together. Our pilgrimage to Iona had certainly changed each one of us and we were all agreed that, over the centuries, God had clearly used this place to touch the lives of countless people. But this change, this transformation, was not about changing people in order for them to become merely more 'religious'; instead, it was about giving them a sense of wholeness and integrity to live the gospel in a different, more authentic way. At every opportunity, this life of wholeness and authenticity shuns the divisions between 'sacred' and 'secular'. It encourages people to seek ways to be more fully present to God, but at the same time to recognise that God is fully present to his people, whether in each other or in the messy stuff of the world around us—that which is political, social, cultural, economic or, indeed, the conventionally religious.

A COMMITMENT TO ECUMENISM

Around St Martin's Cross that evening, we also felt that, as committed Christians, the call to work against division, injustice and isolation in local communities primarily meant working as closely as possible with other believers. It never ceases to amaze me that there are still Christians who honestly believe that it is possible and even acceptable to pray for peace in Iraq and Afghanistan, but at the same time think that the Methodists or the Anglicans or the Roman Catholics or the Baptists or whoever have got it all wrong. Surely the peace of the world begins wherever we are—even with peace in our own hearts—otherwise there is no hope.

In my own life, two things have influenced me in my conviction that striving towards ever closer ecumenical relationships is not a Christian option but an absolute. First, there was the daunting experience of telling my somewhat enthusiastic Roman Catholic grandmother that I wanted to be an Anglican priest—but then she took me by surprise! Her response was simply one of joy, and she had one proviso: she told me that I would have her blessing only if I promised her that I would always greet everyone equally on the street, in the hospital ward or wherever—and not just the Anglicans. That has remained a fundamental principle with me throughout my ministry. The second thing (or, rather, place) that reminds me of the importance of the ecumenical adventure, and how we can go about it, is Iona.

That Iona pilgrimage made a powerful impression on all of us. Those of us who shared the island for a week have kept in touch ever since. It moved me away from a comfortable and passive ecumenism—simply believing it to be part of my Christian vocation, albeit an important part. It took me, and continues to take me, to a place of risky and active ecumenism where there is a costly commitment to the process of sharing fully with other Christians the life of the risen Christ. Similarly, Iona convinced Dylan that knocking on the doors of Presbyterian households, at the very least, was an authentically Christian thing to do, despite some entrenched opposition from his own parishioners. Dylan and I are still in close contact and he is for ever telling me how transforming that shared Iona pilgrimage was for him and the ecumenical community he now serves.

✼

PENNANT MELANGELL: SEEKING WHOLENESS

HARRY AND SUSAN

Harry and Susan had been married for just over a year. Both of them were committed Christians and active members of their local church, which was in the city where they lived. Studying and knowing the Christian faith was very important to them: Harry was one of the Bible study group leaders and Susan a church youth worker. Harry spent hours preparing for the weekly group meeting and had trained as a part-time theological lay pastor on an extramural study programme at a local college. His group was popular and attracted people from nearby churches as well. Similarly, Susan devoted a lot of her time to church youth activities. She led a midweek youth group with four other people, as well as a Sunday crèche. Several times a year, she would arrange to take her group away on a weekend camp where they would link up with groups from other places.

As active lay leaders, Harry and Susan were also members of the church's worship coordinating team, which supported the minister with the planning and conducting of each Sunday service. The team got together every Tuesday evening. In fact, it was at one of the team gatherings that Harry and Susan had first met, some years previously. The church usually attracted well over 300 worshippers every week and included over 100 children and teenagers. It was a very busy and active community, and Harry and Susan were always at the hub of its action; indeed, it was the centre of their life.

However, Harry's promotion at work meant that they had to move to a new area. They found a new home in a small village and, although the ancient parish church was a beautiful building, located prominently at the centre of the village, it was not well attended. Harry and Susan's previous church experience had provided them, and any other newcomer to the church, with a large social network and a natural place to connect with others in order to make friends. When they arrived in the village, they were keen to become part of the local church community, particularly as they had no children and their immediate family lived far away. To their disappointment, they found that it was all very low-key and downbeat, and the doors were only open for an hour on Sundays.

Harry and Susan's evangelical background had encouraged them over the years to think deeply about questions of human existence. Where do we come from? Where are we heading? What is life all about? Who am I? It had taught them about the importance of theological reflection—how to connect faith, as it is revealed through scripture, liturgy and worship, with people's individual lives as well as the wider life of the world. In his study group, Harry was always keen for the members not simply to study a Bible passage as a historical piece of writing but to relate it to their personal situations. Similarly, Susan always tried to show her youngsters that worship could be fun, and the children in her groups were constantly encouraged to see that faith touched every aspect of their lives and not just what took place on Sundays.

In their new church, they found that the members were not at all interested in such an approach. Wider questions to do with faith were not raised and there was a general discomfort about being what the congregation might have described as 'too intense'. On the whole, people were far more interested in the date of the next cake stall at the local market. And so, quite soon after their arrival in the village, Harry and Susan had to confront an uncomfortable set of emotions—spiritual disappointment, a lack of fulfilment and a feeling of emptiness in worship. Although their personal faith remained strong, they were very disillusioned by the community's apparent lack of interest in the deep things of God. However, they were determined to continue to attend the church and search for spiritual sustenance, elsewhere if necessary.

In their previous church, Harry and Susan used to arrange occasional retreats for the youth group to various places and, on the occasion when I met them, they had been invited for a reunion with the group at Pennant Melangell. Not only is Pennant Melangell an important pilgrimage destination; it is also situated in the beautiful hills at the head of the Tanat Valley in mid-Wales, not too far from my own home. On the occasion in question, some of us from my church had planned an early summer pilgrimage for our parish youth group. There were about 20 of us in all, and some of the parents and other adults who accompanied us had prepared a convoy of cars and a generous picnic. After our pilgrimage walk up to the church from the nearby village, we decided that it would be good to have some refreshments before celebrating the Eucharist. When we got to St Melangell's Church, we found that there was already another group present and we sat next to them to eat our sandwiches. Gradually people mingled and the two groups became quite friendly; I found myself sitting next to Harry and Susan and we started to chat. We invited the other group to join us for our celebration of the Eucharist at the end of the afternoon and had a lot of time to continue talking while our youngsters went off to explore the hillside.

THE SHRINE OF ST MELANGELL

Innocence, simplicity and sheer beauty are all associated with the establishment of this remarkable place, as well as the place itself.

Melangell was the daughter of a sixth-century Irish tribal prince, who had arranged a marriage for her that would offer a prosperous and comfortable life. For some time, though, Melangell had felt a profound sense of calling to be a nun and to a life of prayer. The last thing she needed was a husband that she did not love. Subsequently she escaped across the Irish Sea and landed in Wales. Her faith convinced her that God would lead her to a place of safety where she could nurture her vocation and dedicate her life to him. Eventually, she discovered a haven in one of the most beautiful and silent valleys of the Berwyn Mountains in mid-Wales, the place now known as Pennant Melangell.

Two 17th-century transcripts of a lost *Life of the Saints* tell Melangell's story. Legend has it that, one day, she was deep in prayer when a hare disturbed her silence and sought protection under the hem of her dress. The hare was being pursued by the dogs of a hunter called Brochwel Ysgythrog. Brochwel was at that time the prince of Powys, one of the three great pre-Norman kingdoms of Wales—the other two being Gwynedd in the north and Deheubarth in the south. Brochwel followed his dogs and encouraged them to chase after the hare and catch it, but they retreated, refused to attack and allowed the hare its freedom. The prince was shocked to find that the hare had not only managed to escape the dogs but had even sought the protection of a young woman at prayer.

Brochwel was impressed by Melangell's evident holiness and simple life and began to talk to her. She told him the story of her Irish roots and escape from marriage and that she had been living a life of silence, prayer and peace in the valley for 15 years. Brochwel admired her greatly and granted her the valley as a place of refuge for ever. It is said that she remained in the valley for the rest of her life, a further 37 years, during which time she exercised a dual ministry of continuous prayer and of offering protection to all who sought refuge—people and animals alike. Eventually, other women joined Melangell in Pennant; a community of holy women or nuns was established there and her ministry of prayer and protection was shared and developed.

Melangell died some time in the early part of the seventh century and was buried in Pennant, probably within the simple church that would have stood there at the time. Her story continues with the removal of her body some time in the twelfth century and the placing of it in a very splendid shrine. A stone church was built in 1160 with an apse in the east part of the church, covering the shrine, which is commonly believed to be the earliest surviving Romanesque shrine in northern Europe. The place became a sanctuary protected by law, and those who sought healing, refuge and forgiveness there made generous donations to it.

It is probably at this stage that Pennant Melangell became a place of medieval pilgrimage, with the shrine and story of this remarkable woman becoming its main focus. Like so many other popular pilgrimage sites, the shrine was ransacked during the Reformation but, fortunately, not completely destroyed. It is clear that during the 16th century and in the aftermath of the confusion and crisis of the time, the people of the valley sought to hide and disguise the remnants of the shrine within the fabric of the church walls and the lychgate.

New life finally returned to Pennant Melangell during the late 20th century, when extensive renovations took place, restoring not only the shrine and other aspects of the medieval church but also the practice of pilgrimage to this place of sanctuary. Indeed, by the feast of St Melangell on 27 May 1992, the church was reopened for regular prayer and worship and, almost immediately, a rapid growth in pilgrimage traffic developed.

DOORWAYS INTO THE SACRED

As a pilgrimage leader, one of the things I find most striking about these holy places is the way in which so many modern-day pilgrims resonate with the stories connected to them. Just like Pennant Melangell, many places of pilgrimage find their Christian roots way back in the sixth and seventh centuries. The roots may have been developed and made more sophisticated in the medieval period, but their origins are very ancient, and it is in this much earlier period that the foundations of the belief in the power of particular places were set. Philip Sheldrake writes that the sense of place that the people of that era had was expressed beautifully in their belief that the natural world was a doorway into the sacred (*Living Between Worlds*, DLT, 1995). He argues that this was a major hallmark of the Celtic Christian way of theological reflection: the Celts recognised that in certain places two realms, heaven and earth, could come together. The Celts, in fact, made it their mission to seek out such places and rejoiced when they found one where they felt that a meeting between the earthly and heavenly dimensions occurred.

It didn't take long for the conversation between Harry, Susan and me to come round to how spiritually significant some places are. They told me that because things were not working out for them in their new church, they had been invited to join the youth outing to Pennant Melangell with friends from their previous church. As that was a city church, Pennant Melangell was a world apart from the place their friends called home. Several of them, however, recognised that what they encountered at Pennant Melangell could offer them something they had not even known was lacking in their lives. It offered them a powerful sense of the importance of place, of the significance of rootedness and historical connection going back hundreds of years.

Sadly, for far too many people today, the city has become a place of anonymity, somewhere lacking true depth and centre, where human identity becomes fractured and undermined. This is not only a sociological issue but also one that lies at the heart of spirituality. As I chatted with Harry and Susan, we spoke a bit about how the early Celtic Christian tradition recognised certain places as having a healing and energising power. The Celts sensed within this power a place of meeting between the spiritual and the earthly, a place where God could almost be touched. I often wonder whether the feeling that God is absent is the result of not having eyes open and hearing attuned to God's presence. Being still and reflective in places like Pennant Melangell, which have been hallowed by centuries of prayer, increases our opportunities to experience the sacred presence of God in fresh and invigorating ways.

ALMOST TOUCHING THE HAND OF GOD

This rediscovery of some of the central values of the Christian Celtic tradition helps us understand much better what is meant by the 'immanence' of God—the God who dwells in this world as well as above it and beyond it. In many ways, here lie the roots of the Celtic intertwining knot pattern. The Celts felt the very presence of God almost physically woven around their lives. They were conscious of being encircled by him, upheld by him and encompassed by him. In the hymn attributed to St Patrick, the great Irish saint says, 'I bind unto myself today the power of God to hold and to lead.' For the Celtic Christians, God was a close friend, a companion, a guest in the house, almost a physical presence in life whose hand they could imagine touching. This presence was also expressed in the conviction that God was to be found throughout creation—in the physical elements of earth, rock, water, plants, trees and animals.

What is striking about this Celtic sense of the divine presence is that God is to be found both within creation and outside it. There is no blurring of the distinction between the Creator and the created: it is not what some people call pantheism. It is not worship of nature for its own sake but, rather, a wonderful sense that the whole cosmos is a theophany—a revelation of God's glory, God's abiding presence, God's goodness, wonder and creativity; it is panentheism as opposed to pantheism. The Celtic Christians saw God's presence in the sun, the moon and the stars, and pervading the earth. As Saunders Davies, a former Bishop of Bangor, once said, for the Celt, creation is translucent: it lets through glimpses of the glory of God.

Interestingly, of course, this is not a new way of thinking about God. The Old Testament has an abundance of imagery testifying to the dynamic, living, two-way relationship between God and his creation, in which the trees of the field clap their hands and the mountains leap like rams and the hills skip like sheep in praise of their Creator (Isaiah 55:12; Psalm 114:6–8). The Psalms were especially dear to the Celtic Christians and figured prominently in their worship, and they are full of a sense of God's continuing concern for and loving presence in all his creatures. In her protection of the hare, Melangell was following an ancient biblical tradition of caring for the entire and blessed creation that God has made.

In Patrick's address to the daughters of the High King of Tara, who had asked him where God lived, the Irish saint took the opportunity to speak with passion about God's hands not simply encircling and protecting the earth and everything that it contains, but also quickening, enlivening and inspiring it. It was an altogether dynamic picture of God's active presence at the heart of all that exists.

At the same time, although there is a great intimacy in the language of worship used by the authors of the Psalms and those in the Christian Celtic tradition, there is certainly no overfamiliarity in their approach to the essential mystery of God. It is significant that, in the Celtic prayers, there is almost no prayer in the vocative mood—that is, asking God for this or for that directly. Rather, the mood of the prayers is almost always indirect and invocational, calling down the blessings and the protection of God. For the Celts, God was to be approached with awe, reverence and wonder, even though he was intimately involved in his creation.

I remember several of the youngsters in Harry and Susan's group saying that it was difficult to put into words how they felt about their faith and the things of God while in Pennant Melangell. Certainly, most of them felt that the story of Melangell and the hare spoke clearly about a clash between a violent and aggressive world and a way of life that put its trust in the closeness of God. Such a life was characteristically prayerful and quiet, full of compassion and care for the whole of God's creation—even hares! Visiting Pennant Melangell made vivid to them something of the Celtic Christian stress on the immanence of God, that not only is he present and at work in all things but he can be praised and glorified in and through the whole of creation.

GLIMPSING THE DIVINE

In our conversation, Harry and Susan were keen to reflect further on their experience. They felt that it wasn't enough simply to say that being in this special place brought the essentials of the Christian tradition—whether rooted in the Old Testament or the Celtic tradition or even Eastern Orthodoxy—closer. They wanted the experience in some way to touch the core of their being.

Towards the end of the afternoon, my group gathered for an informal celebration of the Eucharist outside, close to the 2000-year-old yew trees in the churchyard. It's hard to imagine that these trees, which continue to grow in Pennant Melangell, were vulnerable young seedlings when Jesus was talking about his future to Peter, James and John over in Palestine. Harry, Susan and their group joined us in worship. I had planned to read the Gospel account of the transfiguration at the service (Luke 9:28–36) and to give a short reflection on that passage. For a number of years, I had been feeling that Pennant Melangell was an experience of transfiguration—an opportunity to glimpse heaven briefly, as Peter, James and John did on Mount Tabor.

I have always believed that one of the most contemporary of all of Christ's earthly experiences was the transfiguration—a grace that is readily available to all of us today. By 'contemporary' I mean that a great many of us can connect with it. Peter, James and John were taken up to the summit of Mount Tabor at a particular crossroads moment in their own lives and in the ministry of Jesus: things were about to change for all of them. As well as glimpsing the divine just for a moment, Jesus and the three disciples were also strengthened and empowered to face what lay ahead. Many people today—and particularly many who go on pilgrimage—know what it is like to be changed, to be transformed, to be altered, to be healed, so that they can move forward and no longer feel the need to look back. When that happens, peace can be made with the past, and that can only be a moment of transfiguration.

THE GRACE OF TRANSFIGURATION

Over our final cup of tea after the service, Harry and Susan were keen to talk more about the gift of the grace of transfiguration. The passage from Luke's Gospel and my subsequent meditation on it had clearly resonated with them in this particular place. Harry said that, for him, in Pennant Melangell, the penny had dropped and that Luke's account of that mountain-top experience all those centuries ago was not simply historical but dynamically connected to the present day. The grace of transfiguration enabled him now to see reality in a different light.

In all the Gospels, the story of the transfiguration occurs about a week after Jesus tells his disciples that they must pick up their crosses before they can follow him. This sets the story firmly in the context of faithfulness to Christ's teaching, for it is only in a life lived in the imitation of Jesus Christ that there can be healing and the opportunity for a renewed and transformed life. The Gospel accounts of the transfiguration reveal both a Christ who was transfigured and a Christ who is transfiguring. Those who choose to keep company with him can thus expect that their lives will not be the same again. Furthermore, the mountain-top experience was not a private affair between three privileged disciples, Christ and two key Old Testament figures, Moses and Elijah. Rather, it became a converting experience even for those left at the foot of the mountain who came to believe in Christ's power to transform, to breathe new life into what was otherwise dull and lifeless.

Harry and Susan recognised that something special had happened to them that day at Pennant Melangell and that their experience was a result of actually being in a particular place—remembering the story of a certain young girl and pausing a while to reflect on their own situation in the light of a Gospel story. How that situation would now unfold for them, they couldn't tell. They were certain of one thing: their time at Pennant Melangell, and all that went with it, would not solve their frustration about their church circumstances back home. But they had learnt to believe that the ordinary can become extraordinary as we seek to be ever faithful to the redeeming and creative God. As we walked back along the single-track road to the cars together, I promised Harry and Susan that I would keep in contact.

LEARNING MORE BACK HOME

About two months after that extraordinary pilgrimage to Pennant Melangell, Harry and Susan came to visit me one Saturday afternoon. They told me that, although they had benefited greatly from our day together in the Tanat valley, it was not until some time after they had returned home that the experience blossomed into full flower.

They told me that they had never realised the spiritual importance of particular physical places until they visited Pennant Melangell. Although they had been on awaydays and weekends with their previous church, it had always been a retreat-based experience: the physicality of place had never had any real significance. At Pennant Melangell, they came to realise the truth that some places are 'thin', in the sense that when you are there you feel closer to God, closer to ultimate meaning, closer to a state of mind that has been transformed by the values of God's kingdom. Previously, the nearest they had been to thinking in this way was in their former church building and in the company of like-minded Christians. Now their attitude had completely changed.

The other significant change that they had experienced as a result of the pilgrimage was the ability to look at their new home situation differently. In their old home, the church had been the centre of their lives, with all the activities and busyness of a large Christian family, but they now wondered whether that was a false sense of belonging. It is as possible to get lost in a busy church as it is to get lost anywhere: there is a danger of getting swept along by the general momentum, so that a sense of perspective becomes blurred. In a city context, too, it is generally (although not always) easier to discover places where social networking is straightforward: for Harry and Susan it was the church. But in a rural setting, it demands more effort, and people have to craft their lives in order to build up social connections.

Their new church was certainly going to involve effort and perseverance, but Harry and Susan both believed that it was not beyond the bounds of possibility to get it to work for the good of all. Who knows but that the transfiguring power of the risen Christ, in partnership with the new strength that Harry and Susan found on their pilgrimage, can provide the energy needed to transfigure this parish church and possibly lead to a much deeper spiritual understanding. After all, if Melangell could befriend hares against all the odds, then anything is possible!

＊

WHITHORN: LISTENING TO THE SOUND OF THE SPIRIT

COLIN

Colin had experienced a stable and supportive childhood but he was a shy person and didn't find it easy to make lasting friendships. Somehow there was always something a bit different about him. It wasn't so much that he was a loner—he always jumped at the opportunity of company—but even in company he seemed to remain alone in his own thoughts. He was an only child and his parents had been well into their 40s when he was born, so as he grew up they were older than most of his friends' parents. Consequently, Colin was much more comfortable in the company of older people and loved to hear their stories of a bygone age, particularly of the immediate post-war years, which sparked his lively imagination. He loved to hear first-hand stories about people making space in their lives for the hope of better times, following the atrocities and destructiveness of war.

As Colin came to the end of his school career, one of his more supportive teachers suggested that he should consider developing his love of books. From an early age, he was an avid reader and showed an almost obsessive devotion to books: he would read them, repair them, cover them, catalogue them and store them. At school he was the librarian's pupil assistant and could always be found in the school library.

Colin's father had a much older sister living in Glasgow, and she offered Colin an opportunity to stay with her for a few months to see if there were any jobs available in the city. By chance, one of the city museums needed a maintenance assistant and the curator attended the same church as Colin's aunt. Colin got the job and it proved hugely successful for him. Although a maintenance assistant, the opportunity in the museum allowed him to take up his interest in books at the museum library and in the ancient manuscript room. However, three months into the job, his aunt died and eventually he inherited her small but comfortable house quite close to the city centre. His parents were too old and too set in their own ways to join Colin and so he found himself living alone for the first time ever.

Initially, the city centre environment proved difficult for Colin because there was no real community there, but he was hungry for contacts and anxious to make the opportunity work. His difficulty with making friends meant that this was going to be a difficult period, though, and the memory of some of his early struggles with shyness and reserve at school came flooding back. Nevertheless, he remained determined to make the most of having a pleasant house and an interesting job in the city. Much of the time, his feelings were mixed: he was grateful, excited, energised and desperate to find community, and he also had tremendous patience, determination and a great deal of hope. Just like those people picking up the pieces in post-war Britain in the stories he remembered from his childhood, Colin felt a sense of challenge in his personal life. Recalling those old stories now energised him; to gain some perspective on his situation, he decided to take a holiday and spend some time in the Whithorn area, as he had heard quite a lot about the history of the area and particularly about the Ruthwell Cross.

My first and only pilgrimage to Whithorn was part of a whistlestop tour of holy places in the north-west of England, as fieldwork research for a book. I wanted to know more about the arrival and roots of Christianity in Britain, and I had decided to stay a week in the Dumfries and Galloway area of southern Scotland, so as to explore Whithorn, see the Ruthwell Cross and pay an overnight visit to the Isle of Man. I had planned to be alone to give myself time and space to write, but it didn't quite work out that way. I was staying in a hotel not far from Whithorn and, over a drink in the bar before supper on my first night, I got talking to Colin.

CHRISTIANITY COMES TO BRITAIN

To understand the significance of Whithorn, it is helpful to pause and reflect a little further on the first coming of Christianity to Britain. The story starts, strangely enough, with a paradox—or, at least, with a conflict of evidence. When we look for archaeological evidence, we find very little in the way of monuments or other remains of Christianity dating from the final years of the Roman occupation of Britain. The material evidence available suggests a strongly flourishing Celtic paganism rather than Christianity. The verbal evidence recorded in some early documents, on the other hand, tells a different story. There is no suggestion, for instance, in the biography of St Germanus, written in the fifth century by his disciple Constantius, that he had to combat paganism as well as refute Christian heresy. Similarly, in the following century, Gildas found it necessary to attack the failings of a mature church that had become decadent, rather than criticise a young group of evangelists. These are positive pointers, showing, despite the lack of archaeological evidence, that the Christian faith was reasonably well established in Britain by the time the Roman army finally left in the year 410.

Reliable traditions about the British martyrs Alban of Veru-lamium and Julian and Aaron of Caerleon show that there were Christian communities in southern Britain before the conversion of Constantine in 311. Less than a year after the Edict of Milan in 312, which commanded that Christianity should no longer be persecuted, there was a strong and vibrant British church hierarchy, as shown by the British bishops who attended five church councils in Europe between 314 and 384. Evidence also shows that they were an educated clergy. Hilary, the Bishop of Poitiers in the mid-fourth century, notes in one document that British bishops had been a great help to him in his attack on Arianism, the heretical doctrine that denied the true divinity of Christ. Also, Sulpicius Severus, a close friend of Martin of Tours, records that some British bishops had benefited greatly from an international fund to help them with travel costs for attending the councils.

So who actually brought Christianity to Britain in the first place? The Roman army, because of their involvement in the various wars and settlements of the period, may well have been the original carrier of the new faith: there can be little doubt that some of the soldiers were Christians. Also, the fact that Britain was situated on important trade routes meant that commercial relations, especially with Gaul, brought about a mixing of people and traditions. Linked to both of these military and economic factors were the immigration and emigration movements: for all sorts of reasons, Britons went to live on the Continent and Europeans settled in Britain. With the gradual development of the church and the establishing of various worship traditions, the veneration of European saints, such as Martin of Tours, became important. One of the carriers of these traditions was monasticism, and it was due, in no short measure, to the journeys of the monks that Christianity gradually took root as a way of life and faith throughout the western parts of Europe, including Britain.

Although our understanding of the shape, character and quality of life of the early British church continues to be defined and redefined by contemporary scholarship, the evidence available points to the existence of a strongly Romanised church, which was most prevalent among the Romano-British elite. It was a church whose language was probably overwhelmingly Latin and whose structure, based on local centres of population, generally reflected the Roman pattern of civic organisation, at least initially. Whatever the shape of this early church, it was sufficiently developed to generate a sophisticated, vibrant and influential religious life.

This church survived until the first half of the fifth century, when, after the withdrawal of Roman forces, Britain came under increasing pressure from vigorous assaults—by the Irish from the west, the Picts from the north and, most importantly, the Germanic peoples from the east. Over a period of time, the territory of the British church sharply contracted in the face of increasing pagan advances. The land to the west and the north of the country, which offered the invaders most resistance because of the generally remote and inaccessible character of the landscape, became a place of retreat for believers. As a result, the early British church began to be cut off from the rest of the world. From the fifth century onwards, Christianity was probably restricted to Strathclyde and Cumbria in the north, through Wales to Devon and Cornwall in the south. It appears that the Welsh part of this early church was keen to maintain, as far as possible, the historic link with the old Roman civilisation and with the Christian religion that Rome had introduced. It is worth noting here that the very term 'Welsh' is an early English word that means 'Romanised Celt'.

NINIAN AND WHITHORN

As we have already seen, a characteristic of the church of this time was the development of monastic communities, influenced by the spiritual practices emanating from the Egyptian deserts. Today, Whithorn is a small fishing harbour in Galloway, south-west Scotland, but in the medieval period it was an important pilgrimage place for European Christians. It was here that St Ninian built a Celtic monastery in the year 397—probably the first monastic settlement in Britain. Bede is the earliest writer to mention Ninian, and he describes him as a holy man who had studied theology in Rome. Bede also says that on his return to Britain Ninian built a monastery made of stone, which came to be known as Candida Casa or 'white house'. At this time, stone structures for churches were unusual in Britain. Two other early writings mention Ninian: one is an eighth-century poem, written at Whithorn, that speaks of Bishop Ninian's miracles, and the other is the biography of Ninian written in the twelfth century by Aelred of Rievaulx, the abbot of a Cistercian monastery in Yorkshire.

Aelred tells us that Ninian was born the son of a Pictish chieftain in Galloway in the year 360. Like Bede, Aelred also speaks about the period that Ninian spent in Rome and adds that he studied theology at the feet of Pope Damasus. These were very exciting times in Rome: Ninian may well have come across figures such as Jerome, the pope's secretary and a great biblical scholar who translated the scriptures into Latin in 384 (a translation known as the Vulgate). We know that by the time of Gildas (547), this had become the official Bible translation of the early British church. Two other influential figures in Rome during Ninian's time were Ambrose and Augustine. Ambrose was the hugely influential Bishop of Milan and the teacher of Augustine, who was later Bishop of Hippo.

Rome was the arena of many of the great theological debates of the early medieval period, and none was more important than the one about the nature of God's grace. The debate was ignited by the statements of another Briton called Pelagius. He was born at about the same time as Ninian and left for Rome in 380, at almost exactly the same time as Ninian. Basically, Pelagius argued that we can achieve salvation and find a place in heaven without God's grace: we can do it alone. In 386, he was ordained a priest in Rome and thus achieved for himself an automatic place right at the centre of the theological conversations that were happening at the time. In 411, Augustine wrote a very important treatise on God's grace and attacked Pelagius, his basic line being that grace was absolutely essential in the process of achieving salvation: we can't do it alone but only through grace. Pelagius was condemned a heretic by the Council of Carthage in 424 and again in 431 by the Council of Ephesus.

Ninian's presence in Rome meant that he became immersed in these controversies and, as a result of them, his theological knowledge grew in depth and sophistication, preparing him to be an important figure in what was about to become the emerging British church. He began his journey back to Britain some time in 395, by way of Gaul, and visited St Martin of Tours. Martin was a crucial figure in the fourth-century European church: he himself had been influenced by the work of John Cassian and, through Cassian, had been introduced to the desert model of monasticism. He was a soldier who became a holy man, a hermit and eventually, reluctantly, a bishop.

The thrust of Martin's unique approach was his complete rejection of the way in which much of the church's life, during the last days of Western Roman dominance, had become superficial and elitist. He was a strong advocate of the need to create much simpler Christian communities along the lines of his understanding of the church in the New Testament and what he had heard was happening in the Egyptian desert. This marked the beginning of a dynamic new era for much of Western Christianity, and Ninian, on his way home to Britain, was greatly influenced by meeting Martin.

Martin's story is one of passion and energy, contagious qualities that proved highly significant in the Western church. Hundreds of churches were subsequently dedicated to his memory and he is depicted, throughout the British Isles, on Celtic crosses as well as several ancient monuments. He is remembered for being a wise and generous church leader whose dynamic leadership of the monastic community he founded inspired many of the key Celtic missionaries, including Patrick, Columba, Samson and Ninian. As Ninian left Gaul for Britain, Martin gave him one final gift—

twelve experienced monks who would help Ninian to establish his monastic dream and were also skilled stonemasons.

THE CANDIDA CASA

Once back in Scotland, Ninian found himself a suitable site on the Mull of Galloway and, with the support of his new community of monks, he began to build a stone church, dedicating it to St Martin of Tours. This was the structure that popularly became known as the Candida Casa or 'Hwit-aern', the White House, because of the whiteness of the stone walls. Almost immediately, and probably because of Ninian's theological experiences in Rome, the monastery in Whithorn became a centre for the study of scripture. As such, it played a major role in the subsequent development of the Scottish and Northumbrian church.

As a result of recent archaeological work in and around Whithorn, it is now possible to trace the outline of a circular monastery dating back to the Celtic period. The dig revealed the presence of countless graves of Christians, as well as artefacts such as shards of glass, pottery and fragments of amphorae, all suggesting lively trading contacts with the Mediterranean world. One of the most exciting discoveries was a pile of building rubble—stones of grey lime coated with a thick layer of calcium carbonate, which would have given the effect of a shiny white building. The foundation wall of a small building constructed of those same stones was also found beneath the west end of the medieval cathedral: this was the discovery of the original Candida Casa.

PILGRIMS TO WHITHORN

Throughout the medieval period, pilgrims flocked to Whithorn— lowly and royal alike. Among the royals, there is evidence that

King Edward II came just before his coronation as an act of both thanksgiving and prayer for his future reign. Robert the Bruce came seeking healing, as did his son David II of Scotland. James III, Margaret of Denmark, James IV, James V and Mary Queen of Scots also made pilgrimages to Whithorn—and in 1982 Pope John Paul II came on pilgrimage, almost 1600 years after Ninian had arrived from Rome!

Over the years, pilgrims have come to Whithorn to pause at a number of important stations that testify to a time of vibrant Christian beginnings. The Latinus Stone, for instance, marks the place of a church and praises a generous God. Along with the Latinus Stone, there are the Kirkmadrine Stones, which are among the earliest Christian monuments in Scotland. Pilgrims also visit St Queran's Well, which is believed to have had particular healing qualities for women and children. Even today, pilgrims continue to decorate the tree that overhangs the well—the clootie tree—with rags and handkerchiefs in the hope that the waters of the well can cure the ailments represented by the 'cloots' or rags. There are also a number of early crosses in the area—those in Monigaff Church, the Kilmorie Cross and the Laggangairn Stones—all testifying to the esteem in which the people held Ninian.

The best example of all the crosses is the Ruthwell Cross, erected in about 680. This cross was originally designed to tell the story of the life and passion of Christ. It was first erected as a preaching cross—a sermon in stone. On its face and sides, pilgrims see the depiction of a number of Jesus' miracles and teachings, John the Baptist, Jesus washing the feet of his disciples, the annunciation, the visitation, the crucifixion and the writing of the Gospels by two evangelists. As a preaching cross, it was designed to mark the spot that had been consecrated for the worship of God and where the sacraments of the church were celebrated. There is also a carving, in Anglo-Saxon script, along the edge of the cross, consisting of sections from 'The Dream of the Rood', a poem possibly written by Caedmon, a Northumbrian poet of the seventh century, which explores the meaning of the crucifixion of Christ.

In addition to the stones and crosses, the area around Whithorn has several historic churches: Wigtown Church, Chapel Finian, Dundrennan Abbey, Glenluce Abbey, Sweetheart Abbey, Barnhobble, St Ninian's Chapel, Sanquhar Church and Lincluden Church. All of these, in different ways, throw further light on those important early years in the establishment of the Christian faith in Britain. Subsequent generations of pilgrims have come to Whithorn to celebrate its historic roots and to draw connections between the activities and struggles of those long-ago Christians and their own lives.

MEETING WITH COLIN

It was the exciting prospect of seeing those white stones that brought me to Whithorn, and I was intrigued by the thought of what the conversation between Ninian and his twelve Gallic assistants might have been. It could have been about the Scottish wet weather but it could also have been about what Martin of Tours would have made of their new construction! It could have included what Ninian heard Pope Damasus say about how the church was developing during those early years following the conversion of Constantine. Or it could have been about Jerome and his skilful translation of the scriptures, a copy of which they had managed to bring with them, with hopes of studying it together once the White House was completed. Or they could have talked about how Ambrose, Bishop of Milan, had influenced Ninian and also Augustine. They could even have shared a dismissive conversation about that other British Christian, the heretic Pelagius, who had got the whole meaning of God's grace so very wrong. Whatever the talk that went on, it was most surely exciting and laid the foundations for future church developments on British soil.

If the thrill of visiting Whithorn, for me, was in taking time to pause and imagine those conversations between Ninian and his supporters, as they first handled the white stones for the building of their church, then Colin's thrill was different. He had read Caedmon's poem in its entirety at the museum in Glasgow and now wanted to see which parts of it were on the Ruthwell Cross. As mentioned earlier, from an early age Colin had always had a vivid imagination—those childhood stories that he had heard about the war had fascinated him—and, over the years since, he found most compelling whatever fired that imagination.

Caedmon's 'The Dream of the Rood' is an imaginative poem voiced by the rood—the cross—itself, and tries to capture in words how the cross felt to be the bearer of the Saviour of the world. Caedmon's rood speaks about the mocking and the mishandling that both it and the one who hung on it had to bear, that first Good Friday. The poem describes how this living, reflective rood saw everything that happened and how it even tried to ease the sufferings of Christ. Colin found this idea, of a cross telling its own story, a mesmerising one and wanted to see it for himself.

REFLECTIONS AT ST NINIAN'S CAVE

When I met Colin on my first night in Whithorn, we found that we both had different things we wanted to see, but we agreed to spend much of our final day together, exploring the old stones and crosses, as well as St Ninian's Cave, and maybe reflecting on what we had seen on our own during the week.

When the last day came, the weather was sunny, so we decided to follow the pilgrim route in the opposite of its traditional direction: that is, leaving Whithorn rather than arriving there, and going south towards the coast. Our walk led us over a hillock, and then we could see the beach where St Ninian's Cave lies. It was quite a risky climb down the cliff edge to the mouth of the cave but, by offering each other the help we needed, we eventually made it safely. The cave has an astonishing quality of silence about it and we found it easy to imagine that this was one of the places where Ninian might have come to find the peace he needed for solitary communion with God. The carved crosses on the walls of the cave—some dating back as far as the eighth century—bear witness to the fact that Ninian was not the only one who sought the silence there. And now we were making our own small mark with our presence in this special place.

During that afternoon pilgrimage, Colin had spoken a lot about how his life in Glasgow had dramatically changed after the death of his aunt. This was the first time he had had to face the experience of living alone. While his aunt had still been alive, she'd introduced him to her church and, although he was not a regular worshipper, he did occasionally attend. During one such recent visit to the church, he had heard a sermon that focused on the Holy Spirit. The preacher had asked the congregation to imagine standing in the wind: you can see the effect of the wind, you can feel the freshness of the wind, you can hear the whistling of the wind, but you can't touch it, hold it, see it or box it in. All you can do is to pause gently to listen to the sound. The preacher had suggested that, in the same way, we should pause to listen to the sound of the Holy Spirit. We can search for the Spirit but will only find him in the way he changes people's lives. We can try to touch the Spirit but will only feel him in the way love is shared among people. We can attempt to listen for the voice of the Spirit but we will only hear him in the way he makes others laugh and sing.

On this very last day, I realised that when Colin said he had come to Whithorn to see the Ruthwell Cross, it was actually an excuse. Like so many young Christians today, he was shy and a little scared at revealing his true reason for being there: he had come to pause, to listen more attentively to the voice of the Holy Spirit, so as to be strengthened to seek the right way ahead for his life. Not all pilgrims are open to talking freely about their faith or about the reasons that have brought them to a place of pilgrimage. Often, it takes time for them even to know for themselves why exactly they have come. Colin was one of these people, but Whithorn and particularly the final day's pilgrimage to the cave helped him to recognise what was going on.

As we sat at the mouth of the cave and enjoyed some refreshments, Colin remarked that the place gave him a strong sense of being on the edge, somewhere where everything—land, sea and sky—merged together. He had discovered in the cave and in what he saw from the cave a kind of metaphor for connection, wholeness and integrity. Understanding this made him confident that things could come together for him in his own life. As I listened to Colin, I thought that he spoke a lot of sense and I was pleased that we had saved this visit to the cave until the last day. As we walked back, we felt a profound sense of peacefulness. As with other places of pilgrimage, I often look back to that time and dip into the memory of it to taste again the peace I discovered there. Although I have not stayed in touch with Colin, I hope that he too has found that the sense of peace and wholeness he discovered at Whithorn has endured over the months and years since.

*

—————— *Chapter 14* ——————

LINDISFARNE: RECOGNISING LIFE AS PILGRIMAGE

KEVIN AND LUCY

Kevin and Lucy were so very happy when their first baby was born. They had been married for just over two years and their dream of being parents had at last been fulfilled, so they were proud and delighted. Both of them came from average family backgrounds— neither rich nor poor—and both sets of parents had worked hard all their lives to provide for their children. Kevin and Lucy had several brothers and sisters and they were all very close. They had known each other since primary school and neither of them could remember a time when they were not friends. Eventually, when they were in their early 20s, they began a relationship and eventually got married. When Lucy told Kevin and the rest of the family that she was pregnant, it was the happiest day of their lives: they had been talking about it for such a long time.

Most of the pregnancy was spent preparing—the nursery, the pram, newborn baby clothes—and, of course, choosing the name. On the whole, Lucy's pregnancy went well and both of them attended antenatal classes as well as the parenting course run by the local Methodist Church. One way or another, it was an idyllic start to their life as parents. They also made several new friends during that preparation period. Often, after the antenatal classes and at weekends, the new group of friends would meet socially and the conversation was inevitably 'baby talk'.

Kevin was a self-employed TV camera operator and he was able to continue work as well as spend quality time with Lucy. For most of their time together, they did a great deal of daydreaming about the future—how lovely life would be, caring for their baby, who would one day go to school and to university, and then get married, and so the pattern of life would extend into the future. Whatever they did and wherever they went, they kept saying that next year there would be three of them. As the birth date drew closer, the prospective parents got more and more excited, as did their whole family.

When the big day arrived, Kevin drove Lucy to the hospital and remained with her during that precious time. Labour lasted the best part of a day and Kevin held Lucy's hand throughout, offering much support and comforting words about all those wonderful days that lay ahead. The actual delivery and the first few hours in hospital were uncomplicated, and, when they at last arrived home with baby Max, it was like carrying into the house the most amazing gift that anyone could ever have received. They carried him so carefully and tenderly and just couldn't bring themselves to lay him down: they simply wanted to hold on to him because he was so lovely, so beautiful.

On the second day, though, baby Max refused to feed from Lucy and seemed to be finding it hard to swallow anything at all. Lucy had so looked forward to breast-feeding her firstborn—but it was not to be. Day by day, things got increasingly worse and the health visitors as well as the doctors were very worried by the situation. The following three weeks were harrowing for the little family and culminated in the discovery that Max had a rare and life-threatening tumour in his throat. The doctors informed Kevin and Lucy that he needed urgent chemotherapy that would affect his mobility, such as it was at this early stage, and his eyesight would almost definitely be impaired. In reality, Max probably had only a few weeks to live and, if the therapy was not successful, all they could do was to offer him palliative care. Kevin and Lucy were devastated and their whole new world came tumbling down. They held Max close and cared gently and meticulously for him. Max died in Lucy's arms when he was exactly a month old. The depths of Kevin and Lucy's grief and loss over the following months can hardly be imagined. As time passed, though, they formed the idea of making a journey—a pilgrimage—to the holy island of Lindisfarne, where they would give thanks for their baby's life, tragically short as it had been.

COMING TO LINDISFARNE

One of the gaps in my knowledge of the church in Britain during the late sixth and early seventh centuries was about church activity in the north-east, so I decided that a pilgrimage to Whitby and Lindisfarne would be beneficial. Whitby was great: I went there with a friend and explored the town as well as the exhibition centre near the remains of the old abbey. I had always been very interested in St Hilda and her role as host of the Synod of Whitby in the year 664. Now it was time to travel a little further and pay my respects to St Aidan and St Cuthbert and their activities in Lindisfarne. It was unusual for me to be there around Easter, as it's not often that a priest can take time off during that period. As it happened, though, I was between jobs and it occurred to me that a short Lindisfarne retreat would be good.

When I met Kevin and Lucy, it was early on Good Friday afternoon and I was sitting on a bank on Lindisfarne, overlooking St Cuthbert's Isle (a smaller island to the south-west). In the distance I could see a group of about 20 people walking across the Slakes—the causeway to Lindisfarne—some of whom were carrying large, heavy crosses. I wondered what was going on, and so I made my way towards them and asked one of the people carrying a cross who and what they were. This person was Kevin, and, as I was by myself, he, his wife Lucy and their friends invited me to share their flasks of coffee and scones. Kevin knew Holy Island well—he had been to the island several times to film there—and he understood the tides and the way back to the mainland. He explained that he, Lucy and their friends were members of the Northern Cross group, who had been walking part of St Cuthbert's Way to Lindisfarne as their annual pilgrimage. I decided I would take up his offer of a walk around the island and learn from his knowledge of this special place. It was during that afternoon that I got to know their story of the loss of baby Max and how important Holy Island was to them as a couple.

As pilgrims approach Lindisfarne, there is a brown tourist information sign that names the place 'The Holy Island of Lindisfarne'—a formula first used by medieval pilgrims. Although it is only truly an island twice a day, because of the incoming tides, Holy Island or Lindisfarne has been a stronghold of Christianity for many centuries, with itinerant monks coming to pray and worship God there since as far back as the seventh century.

AIDAN OF LINDISFARNE

St Aidan, a monk of Iona, came to Northumbria in 635 at the request of King Oswald, who was enthusiastic about converting the native peoples of his kingdom to Christianity. Aidan focused his missionary activities at Lindisfarne and became the first abbot of the island's monastic community and bishop of what had become a large diocese. The original monastery would probably have consisted of small, simple wooden huts built around a central church, with an adjacent public space consisting of a guest house, dining area and, eventually, hermitages outside the boundary walls. Like almost all the other Celtic monastic settlements, this one attracted visitors and pilgrims from the very start. Quite close to Lindisfarne, on St Cuthbert's Isle, the remains of a seventh-century cell and a late medieval chapel have been discovered, and to the south-east lies the island of Inner Farne, where Aidan could well have established his own private retreat.

The influence of Aidan and his group of monks made for rapid and effective growth of the Christian faith in the area. In his history of the church in Britain, Bede relates how Aidan and King Oswald travelled throughout Northumbria: Aidan preached and Oswald translated into the local language. Despite the ravages of war, plague and poverty during that period, Aidan's missionary activity was relentless and determined. Throughout Northumbria, provinces were founded, bishops consecrated, monasteries established and thousands of Christians baptised. The influence of Aidan's Northumbrian monastic foundations was huge. Above all else, it was his Celtic-style monasticism, first learnt on Iona, that precipitated the extensive process of Christian conversion. The monasteries provided Christian education, accommodation, health care, spiritual direction and wise counsel as well as protection.

Women also played an integral part in Aidan's missionary work, and convents for nuns were established along with monasteries that, unusually, housed men and women together. Probably the most famous of these women was Hilda, who initially became the abbess of a convent in Hartlepool. She was of royal lineage and was baptised at the age of 13 by Paulinus, a Roman monk who was sent with Mellitus and Justus by Pope Gregory in 601 as part of the papal strategy to support Augustine in Canterbury. Eventually Hilda left Hartlepool and became the abbess of another mixed monastery in Whitby, where she remained until her death in 680.

Hilda's monastery in Whitby proved to be one of the most important places in the whole of Aidan's missionary activities during the seventh century, becoming a centre for theological learning and artistic skills. One of the lay brothers there was Caedmon, a poet, singer and talented biblical manuscript illustrator. As mentioned in the previous chapter, it was he who probably composed the poem 'The Dream of the Rood', part of which is engraved on the Ruthwell Cross.

CHURCH POLITICS

In the year 664, Hilda hosted an important gathering of bishops, monks, theologians and politicians—the Synod of Whitby. Although the Synod spent some time discussing the correct trimming of the monastic tonsure and baptismal practices, the main impetus behind the gathering were the discrepancies that existed throughout Britain at that time regarding the dating of Easter. Aidan, coming from the monastery of Iona, had used his own community's method and, throughout his mission to Northumbria, encouraged his newly established churches to use that same dating. However, the method of calculating the date of Easter in the south of England and on the Continent was different. King Oswald's son and successor, King Oswiu, presided over the synod. Indeed, he himself had been a victim of these discrepancies: his wife, who was from the south, used one method and he another. While the king celebrated Easter Day, the queen observed Palm Sunday—with all its Lenten restrictions.

The synod, then, was seriously divided on this issue and a resolution was called for. On one side of the divide were those who had been influenced by Aidan's mission (Aidan had died in 651): Colman, Bishop of Lindisfarne; Hilda, Abbess of Whitby; and Cedd, Bishop of the East Saxons, along with their many followers. On the other side were Agilbert, Bishop of the West Saxons; Wilfrid, Abbot of Ripon; Romanus, a priest from Kent; and James, who had been one of Paulinus' deacons from Rome. Those who followed Aidan's dating had been educated in Lindisfarne and those who followed the other method had been educated on the Continent.

Bede's account of the proceedings relates how Oswiu, in his

role as president of the gathering, stressed how vital it was that all Christian people should celebrate their most important festival at the same time. After much discussion, the Continental party won the day and, as a result, Wilfrid was promoted Bishop of York, which replaced Lindisfarne as the episcopal seat. This move ended some of Aidan's tradition, but not all of it, for Lindisfarne continued as a place of scholarship, evangelisation and pilgrimage. Although the Synod of Whitby was a huge turning point in the subsequent relationship between the Celtic and the English church, it took a long time for the churches in the Celtic tradition to accept its decisions.

CUTHBERT OF LINDISFARNE

The other celebrated saint of Northumbria was Cuthbert, who was probably the most significant offshoot of Aidan's mission in the north-east of England. He first entered Melrose Abbey and then, in the year of Aidan's death, moved to become a monk at Lindisfarne. In 661 he was chosen as its abbot and later its bishop. He died in 687 and was buried on Holy Island: in honour of his preaching ministry, the community produced the magnificently illuminated manuscript of the Gospels known as the *Lindisfarne Gospels*, which can be seen today in the British Library.

However, in 875, when Lindisfarne was attacked and pillaged by Vikings, the group of monks known as the Congregation of St Cuthbert opened the shrine of Cuthbert and mingled his remains with those of Aidan. The monks carried this sacred cargo away to a place of safety, first moving it around Northumbria and Galloway, and finally burying it in Durham, where, in 995, they built a church to shelter the new shrine. In 1093, a group of Benedictine monks from Durham returned to Lindisfarne to re-establish a community on the island and consecrated a new church there in 1120. Sadly, just as the Viking destruction had come in 875, so Lindisfarne was again destroyed in 1541, this time by royal command of King Henry VIII, and only three of the great Norman arches of the church remain.

PILGRIMS TO LINDISFARNE TODAY

Today, most of the pilgrims to Lindisfarne come from the north-east of England and are visiting to pay their respects to a place they call their own 'cradle of Christianity', as the members of the Northern Cross group were doing. Unlike many other places of pilgrimage, though, it does not have one particular site where people's journeys come to a climax. Early medieval pilgrims would have had the shrine of Cuthbert at which to pray. They would have brought the needs of their families and friends with them in their hearts and laid their prayers at Cuthbert's tomb. Since the remains of Cuthbert were removed to Durham, Holy Island has had no one major place of gathering, but instead the whole place is suffused with a sense of the divine. On Lindisfarne there is no need to seek the holiness of particular things or particular spots; rather, the island itself offers pilgrims an opportunity to open themselves up to a reality that is far greater than self.

Creating space for people to discover the presence of God lies at the heart of two contemporary religious communities that welcome pilgrims to the Lindisfarne area, and the resources of these communities also offer a great deal to Christians who are seeking fresh and meaningful ways of worshipping in the Celtic tradition. Since the late 20th century, the Community of Aidan and Hilda has drawn people together from many countries to find ways of reconnecting with God in a wounded world. Aidan was chosen as one of the patrons of this community because of his prophetic missionary journey that he shared with others, and Hilda as the other because she nurtured the gifts of an amazingly wide spectrum of people. The modern community, like Aidan and Hilda themselves, represents different genders, nationalities, worship traditions and theological approaches, but also the real possibility of uniting something that was once broken. The community is based in a house on Holy Island called The Open Gate and offers a wonderful ministry of welcome to all pilgrims.

The second religious group in this area is the Northumbria Community, which is based at Hetton Hall, a few miles inland. This community is also a gathering of members from all over the world who seek to rediscover the flame that ignited the hearts and mission of the early monks and nuns in Northumbria. The community operates mainly as local groups meeting regularly for friendship, the sharing of stories and worship. Originally, Aidan, Hilda, Cuthbert and their followers were noted for the way in which their common monastic vocation did not shun the world but, rather, worked tirelessly to proclaim the radical values of the gospel at the heart of the world: this was their mission. The same ideal remains a central part of the vision of the two modern-day communities.

CARRYING THE CROSS

Another modern-day expression of Lindisfarne's spiritual heritage is the Northern Cross group. Every year, various groups of pilgrims begin their walk from across the north of England and Scotland, and, over the course of a week, make their way to Lindisfarne, carrying crosses, singing hymns and praying in different places. They travel as individual groups and very often meet up just off the Slakes, making the muddy walk across to Holy Island together in order to remember the crucifixion of Jesus. What I find particularly interesting is the way the group conducts the pilgrimage: it is as much an act of prophetic witness to the crucifixion of Christ, for those who see them walking, as it is a spiritual nourishment for those who walk the pilgrimage. The group originated in the 1970s when some Christian students sought fresh ways of celebrating Easter, and Kevin's father had been among the founding members. Kevin had been a member since childhood and, for some time, he had also been a member of the Northumbria Community. Some years before, he had introduced Lucy to the Northern Cross group and they had participated in the annual Holy Week pilgrimage to Holy Island many times. Indeed, they had hoped, in time, to bring Max along with them but, alas, that was not to be.

As I walked and talked with Kevin and Lucy on Lindisfarne that Good Friday afternoon, it became clear to me that they were not in a happy place, and gradually they told me their story and about how their beloved baby son had died. They told me how they felt that their life together was now in a strange place, like a drifting boat with no anchor: they explained it in terms of a kind of deep personal exile. Both of them had decided that this pilgrimage to Lindisfarne, a year after Max's death, would be an appropriate and special way to remember him and to thank God for the gift that they had had for such a short time. Lucy said that, although the whole of the walk had been a powerful experience, it wasn't until she saw the posts of the Pilgrims' Way across the causeway and the crosses that they were carrying, weaving their way between those posts and the ruins of Lindisfarne's Priory on the horizon, that she was able to say that this had been the right thing to do.

Unlike many modern pilgrims, the Northern Crossers still travel on foot. Both Kevin and Lucy spoke about the way the physical walk helped them to engage with the rhythm of their lives. The act of walking has a rhythm to it and, as they took each step towards Lindisfarne, and as they breathed each breath, and as they listened to each beat of the heart, they were getting closer to the place where they believed they could pause for a while to remember Max and thank God for his little life. What was important to Kevin and Lucy was not necessarily the distance they had walked but, rather, the reason and purpose for the walk: they were conscious that it was a spiritual act and, at the same time, a tangible and intensely physical experience.

The stinging experience of deep grief is a universal fact of life and, at some stage, it affects each one of us. It pulls us in different directions and initially arouses within us an array of conflicting and strong emotions: doubt, shock, anxiety, despair, anger. But for the first time in my life and my ministry, I realised as I talked to Kevin and Lucy that, whereas the process of mourning has an external feel about it, grief is an entirely internal process. Kevin and Lucy had done their mourning, but they were now on pilgrimage to seek ways of coming to terms with their grief. The hallmarks of such longer-term grief are quieter emotions—sadness, melancholy, depression (which is often described as internalised anger) and loneliness—and each of us has to find ways to allow them full expression.

WALKING WITH THOSE WHO GRIEVE

All too often in pastoral ministry, I have encountered people who think the best way to deal with grief is the fast way—to get on with 'normal' life as quickly as possible. They suppress their grief and encourage grieving people to wear masks so as to show strength and rapid adjustment to the new situation. But grief is neither an illness nor a weakness; nor is it in any way bad. Essentially it is a spiritual process of longing. To hold on to it for too long without releasing it in any way leads to self-destruction, as unexpressed grief can breed emotional and physical illness, fragility and hostility towards other people and the things of life in general. Kevin and Lucy felt that their period of mourning had finished months ago but that their grief now needed an appropriate place and a proper time of expression. It was grief that had kept them in their place of personal exile. They had accepted the reality of losing Max, with all the accompanying pain of that bereavement. They also felt that they were very slowly adjusting to living with the memory of Max as opposed to his bodily presence: again, that brought them pain. The real purpose of their pilgrimage to Lindisfarne was to find strength to live with all of that and to discover ways of reinvesting emotional energy in the future.

The walk with those grieving parents on that Good Friday afternoon taught me so much and revealed another truth about grief that I had never quite recognised before. For Kevin and Lucy, this pilgrimage had been an opportunity of allowing God the chance to walk alongside them, not the other way round. They were inviting him to come and share the bitterness of their suffering through their walk together, so that their pain could be transformed into a source of new life and new direction. I couldn't help but think of the Gospel story about the raising of Lazarus (John 11:1–44). At the tomb where Lazarus had been buried, Jesus commanded the mourners to do two things: to move the stone away from the entrance and to take away the burial clothes that bound his friend. Before my encounter with Kevin and Lucy, I had not fully understood the significance of this double command. It was not Jesus who rolled the stone away and it was not he who loosed Lazarus' grave clothes. Jesus invited the mourners to do these two acts, thus involving the whole of the community in the process of removing the stones of grief, the accoutrements of mourning, that keep all of us in the place of personal exile that is bereavement. Even though we may feel that we are alone in our grieving, there are, in truth, others who can walk alongside us, being the living presence of God for us and eventually helping us to move on.

Lindisfarne was a place where Kevin and Lucy's grief could finally be expressed. It was not the case that their grief could be left here: I don't think for a moment that they wished for that. What they wanted in their pilgrimage was simply space to breathe through their grief, in order to move on together out of exile and into whatever awaited them in the days to come. For me, as for many pilgrims, I happened to be at the right place at the right time with the right people, so that in my encounter with Kevin and Lucy I also discovered something new—a fresh understanding of how to walk with those who grieve. It is all too easy to be caught up by itineraries and deadlines, even on pilgrimage, and fail to see where God is actually at work. Then we miss the opportunities to learn from others through apparently chance encounters. For me, as for Kevin and Lucy, that Holy Week journey was a moment of special grace.

*

—————— *Chapter 15* ——————

YNYS ENLLI: LOOKING TOWARDS THE END

ROBIN

I first met Robin when I was a student. That year, we had one of those rare but lovely hot summers and a group of us from the Anglican Chaplaincy in Bangor arranged to rent a cottage on Ynys Enlli (Bardsey Island) for a week. In fact, it was the first time I had ever stayed overnight on the island; all my previous visits had been day trips. One of my friends had a car and so we drove to Porth Meudwy—the small fishing cove from which the boats depart to the island—where we met the other Enlli pilgrims who were going to share our boat. Porth Meudwy literally means 'hermit's bay', which gives a sense of how important this place has been to the religious history of the island.

As there are no shops or restaurants and not even electricity or mains water on the island, pilgrims and visitors have to take with them all they think they will need for their stay. So Porth Meudwy was bustling on that glorious Saturday morning in late July, and boxes of various foods and drinks, toiletries and other delights were stacked on the quayside. The boat trip from Porth Meudwy to Ynys Enlli crosses a channel of water (known as Swnt Enlli—the Bardsey Sound) about two miles wide, which takes about 20 minutes. That morning, there were ten pilgrims on board the boat: three of us from the Anglican Chaplaincy, a family of four, a nun who actually lived on the island and two other visitors from England, one of whom was Robin.

Once on Enlli, Robin and his friend joined our group for worship and the occasional meal. Our stay on the island proved memorable as we shared so much about our lives and our faith, and the five of us remained in contact for a long time afterwards. Sadly, Robin died from a debilitating illness a number of years after that visit, having been diagnosed shortly after his return and told that he had not long to live. In the light of this terrible news, he was determined to relive the Enlli pilgrimage that we had enjoyed previously. A reunion was therefore planned, which turned out to be an amazing kind of Easter Saturday experience for all of us. Holy Saturday may seem like a strangely empty day but we should remember that it was the time when Christ encountered the sharpness of hell in order to liberate the whole of creation. Knowing about Robin's situation filled us with a strange emptiness; yet, in retrospect, it was equally liberating because the prospect of his imminent death brought to mind the hope of eternal life in the presence of God.

Robin had been a regular pilgrim to Ynys Enlli before our first meeting, and on one occasion he had composed an Enlli prayer walk. On the last day of our reunion pilgrimage, the five of us walked the prayer stations together and, as we paused at each of the stops, Robin led a short but extremely powerful meditation. The experience was challenging, exhilarating, fulfilling, but at the same time achingly poignant because of his terminal illness.

We returned to Porth Meudwy having been transformed as a group of pilgrims, and I'm convinced that it was this pilgrimage that helped to give Robin the courage and strength to die in the way he eventually did.

YNYS ENLLI

Ynys Enlli—literally 'the island of the tides'—has been an important place of pilgrimage throughout the Christian history of Wales. It is one of the largest islands off the Welsh coast and, with its mountain, sea cliffs, beaches and lowland area, it provides a variety of habitats for some exciting wildlife as well.

The historical background to its Christian story begins with a monk called Cadfan, who founded the earliest Celtic monastic settlement on Enlli in the mid sixth century. However, many of the island's historians claim that it was almost certainly a place of spiritual significance even in preChristian times. The outlines of the foundations of small round huts dating from the Late Bronze Age (around 800BC) can be seen in the winter or early spring before the bracken grows, situated in reasonably sheltered positions on a level plateau with strategic views of the sea in three directions for protection. Cadfan also founded the church at Tywyn—just across Cardigan Bay to the south-east—and both places claim to be the burial place of this saint.

It was some time during the middle of the fifth century that a large company of Britons arrived in Wales, having sought refuge in Armorica, Brittany, in the aftermath of the departure of the Romans. Cadfan was among them and, according to Welsh tradition, a large group of Christians accompanied him on this journey, namely Padarn, Tydecho, Maelrys, Cynon, Mael, Sulien, Hywyn, Tanwg, Llywen, Tegai, Llechid, Meilir, Cristiolus, Ilar and Rhystyd. Churches bearing the names of all these men are scattered across north-west Wales today.

The earliest record of a monastic presence on the island is suggested by an inscription on a stone originally found at the foot of Anelog Hill, on the mainland, and now housed in Aberdaron Church. This records the burial of 'Senacus the Priest together with many brethren' and it probably dates from the sixth century. Early

Welsh monasticism, like that of Ireland, was strongly influenced by fourth-century Egyptian models that gave prominence to both the hermit and community life as ideal forms of radical Christian commitment. It is likely, I think, that Enlli may well have become the focus for such spiritual experiments during the sixth century, attracting those who wished to enter a more rigorous and solitary form of monastic life as a retreat or even as preparation for death.

The monastic settlement on the island must have suffered severely during the ninth and tenth centuries from Viking invasions. Indeed, the English name for the island, Bardsey, is of Norse origin, meaning 'Bardr's Island'. But by the twelfth century it was already a long-established place of special significance in Welsh religious life. Giraldus Cambrensis, in his tour of Wales (1188) with Baldwin, the Archbishop of Canterbury, says that it was the home of 'Culdee' groups—part of the ninth-century Irish monastic reform movement.

THE 'ROME OF BRITAIN'

As part of the restructuring of Llandaff Cathedral and to celebrate the new Norman presence in Britain, Bishop Urban commissioned the publication of a special book in about 1120: the Book of Llandaff. It is in this book that we read the first reference to 20,000 saints being buried on Enlli. In particular, a section of the book is devoted to the life story of Dyfrig or Dubricius, one of the most important founders of monastic life in Wales during the sixth century. He established many religious houses in what are now Herefordshire, Gwent and the Wye Valley, and also had jurisdiction over Caldey Island (off the Pembrokeshire coast). Dyfrig died on Enlli and was buried there, although during the twelfth century his remains were taken for reburial in Llandaff Cathedral in order to give more credibility to the Norman establishment there.

The Book of Llandaff also records that, because of the growing popularity of Enlli as a place of pilgrimage, it became known as the 'Rome of Britain'. Interestingly, there is a longstanding tradition in Wales that three visits to Ynys Enlli are worth one visit to Rome! One 19th-century writer states that William Bodwrda, a Welshman from the Llyn Peninsula but living at St John's College in Cambridge in 1640, used to tell students that Enlli was to the Welsh what Westminster Abbey was to the English. He said that Enlli was an island of indulgences, absolution and pardon—the road to heaven and the gate to paradise. He also claimed that he had once met another Welshman called Griffith Roberts, who was a Canon of Milan Cathedral and had told him that he had seen a charter of Enlli under the hand of 'the pope of Rome' that granted great indulgences to those who made pilgrimages to the island in honour of the 20,000 saints buried there. What a tragedy it is that William Bodwrda failed to record which pope was the author of the charter!

Modern-day pilgrims can still see the remains of the 13th-century abbey of the Augustinian monks who took over the ancient Celtic foundation. The monastery was destroyed in 1537 during the Reformation, but Christian faith and worship continued on the island through the centuries and flourished especially in the 19th century, when the inhabitants were influenced by the evangelical revival that swept through Wales.

The island was bought by a charitable trust in 1979 and today it is a working community with a small year-round population. Its land is farmed in a way that balances sensitive ecological and environmental goals with modern agricultural techniques, and most of the houses are let to summer visitors. The trust maintains the island as a place to come for spiritual renewal as well as a centre for ornithology, marine biology and other natural sciences.

PRAYER-WALKING WITH ROBIN

As a regular pilgrimage and retreat leader on Enlli, one of the comments I hear most often from pilgrims is that the accumulated prayer over the centuries on the island is almost tangible. Certainly the place gives itself freely and abundantly to those who seek to pray, and there are many spots that provide space to do this: a chapel, a ruined abbey, an oratory, a well, cliff edges, beaches, mountain-top, open spaces and hidden niches here and there. They all invite us to join in the prayers of those Christian pilgrims who have sought God here for almost 1500 years and to join in what we might think of as the island's own prayer—the wordless, indefinable (yet somehow real) link between creation and Creator.

When Robin led us on his prayer walk around the island on our final day together, we paused to pray at nine different locations. We began with an opening prayer:

O God of our journey, its beginning and its end,
source of our longing and heart of our hope,
be beside us here where you have been before,
go ahead of us now and lead us
by the hand deep into your heart.

After we had prayed this prayer together, we walked silently towards the small quay where the boats arrive. It's here that some pilgrims arrive on Enlli for the first time and where others arrive at a place that feels like home because they have been coming for so many years.

For me, the ending of that opening prayer was striking: it remained with me throughout that memorable day and, indeed, has stayed with me ever since. Over the years—and in this book—I have said a lot about how the whole of life is like a journey and a pilgrimage, and how, as we journey to places such as Enlli and Iona and Lindisfarne, these individual pilgrimages can come to represent our lives in microcosm. Robin summed that up for me as he prayed that God would clasp our hands firmly and nudge us gently into the depths of his own heart—the heart of all being, the heart of creation. Hearing those words that day encouraged me more than ever to start listening attentively to the heartbeat of God. As a pilgrimage leader over the years since then, I have had the privilege of helping others begin to explore how they too can become attuned to God's heartbeat in what they encounter around them. Indeed, one of the marks of an authentic pilgrimage destination is that claims will have been made, over the centuries, that the place reveals God's heartbeat in some special way. If that experience is real, as the pilgrims return home they will find that they continue to hear the heartbeat again and again and again in the ordinary routine of life.

Station one: the Cafn (quay) and the boathouse

As we stood together at the landing stage, I couldn't help but feel that the ancient pilgrims, who worried less about health and safety, would probably have landed all over the shores of this island. These days, the sheltered bay comes as a relief to many after what is often a rough boat trip across the sea. The 17th-century churchmen mentioned earlier, William Bodwrda and Griffith Roberts, both referred to Enlli as the gateway to paradise. As modern pilgrims, we were now at the very gateway to Enlli—its threshold, where pilgrims move from sea to land and look back at the bay and the sea and the boat. At the start of any pilgrimage, pilgrims are encouraged to look back either at their lives or to some recent event and hold that memory before God, either in gratitude or in search of healing.

Robin prayed with us: 'Loving God, loving and strong, loving and gentle, pour mercy on us,' and we then spent a while looking out to sea, lifting up those things from our past that we wanted to thank God for. I certainly had much to be grateful for, but, like so many pilgrims, I also had things that needed some dusting and repair work. I recall that I found myself feeling grateful even for those things, because in circumstances of struggle, challenge and even despair, lessons can still be learnt. For a moment, the silence we shared that morning was a heavy silence, probably because we all felt the same way, but it was also a good silence because it helped us clear our minds and set us on the pilgrim way. As we moved on, Robin asked us to pray for all pilgrims, for all who search for a place of depth and prayer, all who seek the fuller life.

Station two: the lighthouse

With our backs to the sea, we turned left and headed towards the lighthouse, going around the bay and on to the small peninsula at the south of the island. The lighthouse is now automated but, for those who sleep on the island, its presence still dominates the night. We walked in silence and the groaning sound of dozens of seals basking in the morning sun was clearly audible, a reminder that we shared Enlli with so many other members of God's creation. Indeed, we share all of life with one another in different ways, and, as we reached the lighthouse, it was this sense of sharing, brought to mind by the seals, that was uppermost for me. On that particular morning, I was privileged to be sharing in a pilgrimage with four people, each of whom was special to me, and I wondered how we would reveal God to one other as the day progressed.

At the lighthouse we prayed those words again: 'Loving God, loving and strong, loving and gentle, pour mercy on us', and Robin read some words from one of T.S. Eliot's poems, 'The Rock'. The poem speaks about the light that is invisible, the light that lightens the way for all God's creatures and the Light that we worship. The chorus speaks of how we see the light but cannot fathom its origins. I found those words challenging because, like so many people, I have always been keen to establish where things come from. The Welsh tend to have a fascination with people's origins and I often find myself asking visitors to my church where they have come from before anything else. I think it's to do with working out connections and wanting to root people in particular contexts. But in his brief meditation at the lighthouse, Robin showed us that it is not always possible to know or understand the origins of everything, and that contentment sometimes rests in simply accepting what we see and being grateful for that.

After a short silence, we picked up our bags and headed towards a black rock in the distance. As we walked slowly and quietly along the shore, Robin asked us now to pray for seafarers and fishermen and all who worked at night.

Station three: Maen Duw

Maen Duw—God's Rock—is the rock at the very end of the island, which is cut off when the tide is high but can be reached with great care at other times. From Maen Duw, pilgrims look out across the seemingly endless expanse of the Atlantic Ocean. For those of us on the prayer walk, it was now coffee time and we sat on the rock enjoying the sea and the sight of more seals.

After coffee, Robin shared an old story about an Englishman abroad who had taken with him a lot of luggage and needed help to carry his bags. He and his hired helpers had been travelling for a few days when the helpers stopped and refused to go any further. When the Englishman questioned them, they told him that they felt they had been travelling so fast that they had left their souls behind. In order to allow their souls to catch up, they needed to pause and rest a while. Since then, I have used that story with pilgrims in many places. When I bring people to Maen Duw, I connect it with the experience of looking out to sea. For the early Christians, such as Cadfan, searching for a place of retreat was a priority. Cadfan would have looked out from his monastery in Tywyn, across Cardigan Bay, and would have seen an island— Enlli—decided to head for it in a coracle and established it as his place of deep retreat. All of us need such places, to think, to pray, to put things into perspective, to escape, to rest and to allow our souls to catch up with us in our frenetic and fast-paced world.

Once again Robin led us in prayer: 'Loving God, loving and strong, loving and gentle, pour mercy on us.' We then set off towards the next station and, on our way, we were asked to pray silently for all those who felt they had left their souls behind, for space to be still, to wait and to be silent.

Station four: the birdwatchers' hide

We walked right along the edge of the island to the northern end, with the mountain on our right and the sea on our left. Because of the slow and gentle pace of the walk, I noticed the rocky shore, the fields and the dwellings on the island as I had never really noticed them before. Eventually we reached a low birdwatchers' hide among the rocks—a covered hut with a long narrow window overlooking the sea. This is a popular place for the many birdwatchers who come to Enlli but it is also a fine place for a long, still watching of the sea, especially in rough weather.

Robin invited us to say the Lord's Prayer together and then he said alone: 'Loving God, loving and strong, loving and gentle, pour mercy on us.' Sometimes, saying a prayer aloud and alone on behalf of others makes those who hear it concentrate more: I certainly did that day.

Robin read one of R.S. Thomas' poems, 'Sea-Watching'. R.S. Thomas was once a regular visitor to Enlli and, as the vicar of Aberdaron, was the island's parish priest for several years. He was also a very keen birdwatcher. As I listened to the poem, I was reminded of the Manx shearwaters that nest on Enlli every year. There are now no rabbits on the island—they all died of myxomatosis in the 1970s—but their warrens remain and every spring the shearwaters take up residence in them. Shearwaters are amazing birds: after laying their eggs in the old warrens, they feed their young on the fatty fish that the seas around Enlli yield in abundance. In June, the adult birds fly off in the direction of South America and then towards the islands of the South Atlantic, leaving their young ones behind. Now the amazing thing is this: the young shearwaters fly off together a couple of weeks later, as and when they feel ready. Unlike the adult birds that have made that transatlantic journey before, for the young ones it is their maiden flight. How can they possibly know the way?

As I looked out to sea from the birdwatchers' hide, I was struck by a similar thought about human beings as adults and as children. Like the young shearwaters, we are fed and nurtured as we grow and mature until we are ready to make our maiden flight. I thought of the many people who had influenced and guided me over the years of my life up till that day, and how much I owed them for all they had given me.

Before setting off on the next leg of our pilgrimage, Robin asked us to pray especially for those who watched and waited for others, those who had no one to watch for them, and for the lonely, the isolated and the sad. We were now heading for the ruins of the abbey and, instead of walking in silence, we were now invited to talk about how we were feeling at this midpoint in the walk.

Station five: the Abbey ruins

The ruins of St Mary's Abbey date back to the 13th century, as mentioned earlier. It was the Augustinians who brought Latin Christianity to Enlli and linked the religious activities of the island with church life in the rest of Christendom. It was they who inherited the Celtic Christian tradition and continued to proclaim the presence of the risen Christ in the world through the long tradition of island monasticism. The ruined tower is still used for worship by many contemporary pilgrims. For us on our prayer walk, it was almost lunchtime and it seemed appropriate to eat our picnics around the Celtic cross in the old cemetery that commemorated the 20,000 saints. Before doing so, we went into the ruined tower and celebrated the Holy Eucharist together.

As the five of us were all young priests, not long ordained, we celebrated the Eucharist together, which was a moving experience. I think we were all conscious, although none of us said so, that this would be the last time Robin would pray on Enlli. The poignancy of both the moment and the act was brought home as he used part of the twelfth-century deathbed poem by Meilyr Brydydd as his meditation. As mentioned earlier, in the poem, Meilyr Brydydd prayed that as he approached his own death, his soul would eventually find its 'place of resurrection' here, on what he called the 'fair island of Enlli'. What was going through Robin's mind at that time? Whatever it was, Enlli certainly seemed to energise and strengthen him to face his own journey in what was left of life.

After lunch we headed in silence in the direction of the well and, as we did so, we were asked to pray for all those who lived on the island, those who cared for it today and for its future.

Station six: the well

We walked behind Ty Capel—the house adjacent to the 19th-century Methodist Chapel—and the chapel itself, and followed a little path partway up the mountainside to one of the island's wells. The well is covered and framed with stone slabs; its water, gathered from the mountain, is crystal clear and is even piped to some of the island's houses. We were invited to look for the mysterious little human face that is carved in the rock above the well.

While Enlli is the destination point for pilgrims who travel there from many different places, it is also intimately connected to two pilgrimage routes on the Llyn Peninsula—a northern route and a southern route. Today, along both coastal routes, there is a string of interesting pilgrimage churches, many of which have holy wells: Clynnog Fawr, Llanaelhaiarn, Pistyll, Llandudwen, Llangybi, Llanbedrog, Llanengan and St Mary's Well right at the tip of the peninsula. These wells would originally have served a dual purpose, providing refreshment and a place for the renewal of baptismal vows. Over the years, they also acquired the reputation of healing particular illnesses.

As we sat around the well, Robin spoke about the water that refreshes the soul, and he read the passage from John's Gospel about the meeting between Jesus and the Samaritan woman at Jacob's well (John 4:5–26). It was here that Jesus was first revealed as the Saviour to the Samaritans and where he spoke powerfully about drinking ordinary water and quickly becoming thirsty again. But as we drink his water—his energy, his word, his sacraments, his compassion—we will never become thirsty again; nor will we tire of sharing that water of life with all those we encounter.

As we prepared to leave the well, Robin asked us to pray for those we ministered to as clergy, and to name those we wished to remember at the well. We then sang a couple of Taizé chants and once again we prayed together: 'Loving God, loving and strong, loving and gentle, pour mercy on us.' We got up and moved away from the well, this time praying for those who were literally thirsty and hungry and also for those whose hunger and thirst is for justice.

Station seven: the cave of St Elgar

We followed the wide track that rises up the mountainside, halfway along to our right, and behind a rock we found the low cave that was the next station on our walk. Some people call this Merlin's Cave because, as with so many of the islands off the shores of Britain, there is an Arthurian myth or legend connected to it. Some have even suggested that Merlin buried the ancient treasures of King Arthur here on Enlli. But we preferred to think of it as St Elgar's Cave.

During the 1970s, when the Franciscan friars played an important role in the spiritual life of Enlli—serving as chaplains during the summer months—one of their friars, Brother Ramon, prayed in this cave and spoke about the important influence it had on his life. In the twelfth century, when Bishop Urban sought the bones of Dyfrig in order to authenticate his new cathedral's national and spiritual identity, it was Elgar, a hermit of Enlli, who identified their whereabouts. The story of Elgar is recorded in the Book of Llandaff and, as we paused at the mouth of this cave, I wondered whether this was actually Elgar's hermitage: I think Brother Ramon thought so.

At this prayer station, Robin suggested that we should dispense with the usual silent meditation and discuss what we knew of contemporary hermit life. We shared stories about hermits we had known and knew of that day, and particularly those who continued to visit Enlli and lived on the Llyn Peninsula. As we prepared to move on to the eighth station, Robin prayed: 'Loving God, loving and strong, loving and gentle, pour mercy on us.' As we walked away from the cave, we prayed for all those who had dedicated their lives to God in this way and also those who were in the process of discerning a call either to such a life or to ordained ministry. We remembered especially those who worked as spiritual directors and we thanked God for those who walked the spiritual path with each one of us.

Station eight: the mountain top

We climbed the rest of the way to the top of the mountain. This is about 500 feet above sea level and affords beautiful views of the Atlantic and of Cardigan Bay, the mountains of Snowdonia, the whole of the Llyn Peninsula and, on a clear day, the Wicklow Mountains in Ireland. It was getting late by now and the sun was sinking to the western horizon: the sunset on Enlli can be spectacular, and it was on that particular evening.

Our prayer on the mountain top was one of thanksgiving for a wonderful day, for what we had shared together and for the opportunities we had had to pause and reflect on our own situations. We felt that we had grown that little bit closer to each other, to God and to the natural world around us. There at the top of the mountain we felt that we could see the infinity of God's creation and the infinity of his ongoing creative and redeeming work in the life of the world, as well as in the lives of individuals. I was reminded of the fact that, so often, all we need to do is to open ourselves to that infinity and be prepared to say 'Yes' to God's invitation to share our life's journey with him.

Before beginning our descent, one of us read aloud the account of the transfiguration (Luke 9:28–36). We all agreed that we could identify with Peter, who wanted to make the ecstasy of transfiguration last for ever by building three booths, one for Jesus, one for Elijah and one for Moses. In fact, we realised that those booths had already been built for us by Jesus and that by accepting his invitation to be his disciples, we could dwell continuously in those booths of the heart. Certainly, like the experience of Peter, James and John, the descent from our own mountain of transfiguration was a moment of strengthening grace to face the future with renewed energy (an insight that we have also considered in relation to Pennant Melangell). We were also aware that although we did not know what the future held for any of us, we did know who held our future—a truth mentioned elsewhere in this book because it has remained of fundamental importance to me over the years. In some ways, this attitude could be seen as quite risky, but, as Bishop Andy John said a while ago in a Radio 2 'Pause for Thought' broadcast, faith is the act of taking generous risks.

As we prepared to move down the mountain, Robin prayed on our behalf: 'Loving God, loving and strong, loving and gentle, pour mercy on us.' He asked us to think prayerfully about all who cared for the earth and sought to cherish and protect it, and we also gave thanks for the sheer beauty of creation.

Station nine: the road

Although strengthened—transfigured—we made our way back towards the abbey ruins with mixed thoughts because we knew that the pilgrimage was nearing its end. We stopped at a junction where the road heads down to the Cafn, where the boat would take us back to the mainland next day. In fact, this is the only road on the whole island and one that has been walked by many thousands of pilgrims down the ages. As the only road, for some pilgrims it is the way home and for others it is a way forward. Robin read aloud 'Roads go ever ever on', a poem by J.R.R. Tolkien that uses the image of a road going on and on, through different terrain—rocks, trees, dark caves, streams, snow, grass, stones, moonlit mountains. While the changing scenery of life may feel a bit like that, I learnt on that remarkable Enlli pilgrimage that the real worth of any pilgrimage, any journey, is in its return to everyday reality at the end.

As part of our closing devotions together, we read aloud another of R.S. Thomas' poems, 'Groping'. Here the poet describes return as a process of moving away from the boundaries of one's self and into the centre of the heart. There at the centre in the presence of God, it is possible to find the strength and the spiritual compass we need to go forward with faith and in trust.

As we finished our Enlli pilgrimage, we prayed together: 'Loving God, loving and strong, loving and gentle, pour mercy on us' and exchanged a sign of the peace of God before returning quietly to the house where we were staying to spend one final night.

We went back to our different homes the following morning and, just a few months later, Robin died.

❋

AFTERWORD

I started this book with the assertion that the church in the developed world is on the brink of forgetting its defining story. This is the story, revealed to us through the witness of the Bible, about God's ongoing creative and redeeming activity, in which he constantly invites his people to join with him. Throughout the Bible, we see how God makes a covenant with his people as an enduring sign of his faithful commitment to us, his resolve to enter into a deep and lasting relationship with us. It is in this way that he asserts his identity as a relating God and not in any way an isolated one, divorced from the world and its affairs.

This is the story that the prophets were so anxious for the Jewish exiles in Babylon to remember. Many of the exiles lamented that their God had opted to become distant, hostile and even invisible to them while they suffered the disgrace and inhumanity of being taken as prisoners into a foreign and godless land. The challenge that faced Jeremiah, Ezekiel and Isaiah was that, in spite of the many appearances to the contrary, God was still searching for ways to reveal himself anew, even while his people struggled to make sense of life far from home (Ezekiel 37:13; Psalm 139:7–12; Isaiah 40:28–31).

The act of remembering the story of God's close relationship with the human race and his constant renewal of his covenant with us is a central part of our life of faith. Memory is so fundamental to our being human that we would not be able to function without it. It is also at the heart of our sense of identity. Without memory, I could not be I and we could not be we: men and women would be unable to recognise each other or even themselves. From a faith perspective, to remember the story of God's creative and redeeming life, as well as his invitation to us embedded within that story, is at the root of what it means to be human and also to be church.

Over the course of this book, we have moved from the idea of exile as a metaphor for understanding the state of the church, and into the experience of pilgrimage, and we have seen how God's story weaves itself into our own very personal stories. In the act of pilgrimage, we not only grow closer to each other and become more in touch with our own lives, but we recognise the extent of our intimate covenant relationship with God—and how that can bring about a radical purification of ourselves and a healing of memory.

Ultimately, it is in this weaving together of our life with God's life that we are able to discover our proper identity as human beings. Irenaeus of Lyons, one of the first great theologians of the Western church, once said that the true glory of God is to be seen in men and women living life authentically and to the full, and that authentic life is the true vision of God. By living with a pilgrim consciousness—recognising that God is our beginning and our end, and that the physical journey of human living is a pilgrimage from God, which will ultimately take us back to God—we can begin to understand why we were created, the reason for our very being. In this way, the pilgrim can come to recognise that all of life is constantly flowing towards the presence of God, towards an end that really has no end. Pilgrimage is ultimately about progressing into the heart of God. It is about journeying together into God's call to perfection and into a fullness of life that can only, because of the very nature of its being by God's own generous invitation, constantly grow as a deep response to divine grace.

The fast and greedy pace of the world will always stand in the way of this process of spiritual maturing. To grow in faith and hope cannot, by definition of the age we live in, happen naturally. It cannot and never will happen when people insist on moving at a pace that is out of sync with their souls. Again and again I have seen how pilgrimage encourages people to slow down, turn towards God and recognise in him an infinite source of faithfulness, hope and love—the signs of true covenant. All too often, though, this kind of measured and authentic living is threatened by people's becoming less trusting of others, less committed to relationships, less hopeful about the future, more pessimistic about matters of faith and far more cynical about the very existence of God. Only by being rooted and grounded in the story of God's creative and redeeming work will we find growth and renewal of faith. Unless pilgrims know at least some of the story before they begin their journey, they will struggle to understand the story fully—and themselves in relation to the story—when they arrive at their destination.

In Christ we are invited to enter into a covenant in which freedom and fulfilment come as a result of knowing and loving God. Without this spiritual dimension, we will stay trapped in a superficial existence, one that twists and suffocates countless lives simply because so many people try to live in a world of time and space as if that were all that mattered. The temptation is not only to be contented with a mediocre way of being, but to live as if we are on this earth for ever and can behave towards each other, and the planet, as if they are not finite resources.

In the depths of God's grace, we know that the gift of true gospel living is embracing the knowledge that we already live as part of God's kingdom here and now. All the Gospels show us that as a covenant people, we already have one foot in the kingdom and are able to anticipate here on earth the joys of heaven. But none of this is strictly our own, to be kept as private property; rather, it is a gift to be shared. For it is only when this gift of grace is truly recognised, celebrated and shared that it can offer life and nourishment to our arid and starving world—and to our tired Church that is nevertheless eternally beloved of God.

TIME FOR REFLECTION

Meditations to use through the year

Ann Persson

It is not easy to switch from activity to stillness, from noise to silence, from achieving to letting go, from doing to being in the presence of God. This book of biblically rooted meditations provides accessible and practical routes to exploring prayer as that way of being in God's presence, letting the sediment of our lives settle so that we may have a true reflection of ourselves and of God within us.

Loosely based around the seasons of the Church year and also drawing inspiration from the seasons of nature, the meditations range from short 'spaces for grace' to longer exercises that can form the basis for a personal quiet day or retreat.

ISBN 978 1 84101 876 8   £8.99
Available from your local Christian bookshop or, in case of difficulty, direct from BRF using the order form on page 207. You may also order from www.brfonline.org.uk.

WRITING THE ICON
OF THE HEART

In silence beholding

Maggie Ross

In *Writing the Icon of the Heart* we are invited to share the reflections of one who, over the years, has spent long hours in silence and prayer in one of the world's most wild and solitary landscapes, as well as the more urban context of Oxford. Casting new and often startling light on ancient texts and long-established spiritual practices, Maggie Ross shows how faith cannot be divorced from an outlook characterised by a rigorous questioning and testing of assumptions, and a passionate concern for the created world in which we are blessed to live.

This is a book that challenges as well as inspires, and takes us deep into what it truly means to worship, to love, to pray—and what it means to be human, made in the image of God.

ISBN 978 1 84101 878 2   £6.99
Available from your local Christian bookshop or, in case of difficulty, direct from BRF using the order form on page 207. You may also order from www.brfonline.org.uk.

THE JESUS PRAYER

Simon Barrington-Ward

The Jesus Prayer has been known and loved by generations of Christians. Originating in the Orthodox Church, it is a way of entering into the river of prayer that flows from the heart of God, as Jesus continually prays for his people and for the world he loves. Within us, too, the Spirit of God prays 'with sighs too deep for words', and the Jesus Prayer can help us to join in the loving intercession of God-in-Christ for the redemption of all things.

In this revised edition of a BRF classic, Simon Barrington-Ward teaches us how to use the prayer, and provides biblical and historical background for understanding its significance.

ISBN 978 1 84101 588 0   £5.99
Available from your local Christian bookshop or, in case of difficulty, direct from BRF using the order form on page 207. You may also order from www.brfonline.org.uk.

SEASONS OF THE SPIRIT

One community's journey through the Christian year

Teresa Morgan

'"Watch and pray." Advent's motto is good for Lent, too. But I am too tired to pray; even the short step into silence seems a marathon. I am tempted to sit down under the chestnut tree and hope that the new life which touches it one sunny morning will quicken me too. Instead, I turn homewards...'

This book is a journey through the seasons of the year and also through the high days and holy days of the Church. In the company of saints present and past, we travel from Advent Sunday to Advent Sunday, looking for the kingdom of heaven and reflecting on the many ways in which God's love reaches out to embrace and transform the world. Interspersing prose with poetry, this is a book to read slowly and reflectively, stilling our minds to the rhythms of grace and opening our hearts to the peace that passes all understanding.

ISBN 978 1 84101 710 5   £6.99
Available from your local Christian bookshop or, in case of difficulty, direct from BRF using the order form on page 207. You may also order from www.brfonline.org.uk.

WORKING FROM A PLACE OF REST

Jesus and the key to sustaining ministry

Tony Horsfall

Exhaustion, burnout, tiredness, even breakdown... sadly, such conditions are all too common these days, not least among those involved in some kind of Christian ministry, whether full-time, part-time or voluntary. In striving to do our utmost for God, we can easily forget that there were many times when Jesus himself was willing to rest, to do nothing except wait for the Spirit's prompting, so that he demonstrated the vital principle of 'working from a place of rest'.

Drawing on extensive experience of training and mentoring across the world, Tony Horsfall reflects on the story of Jesus and the Samaritan woman to draw out practical guidance for sustainable Christian life and work.

ISBN 978 1 84101 544 6   £6.99
Available from your local Christian bookshop or, in case of difficulty, direct from BRF using the order form on page 207. You may also order from www.brfonline.org.uk.

GROWING A CARING CHURCH

Practical guidelines for pastoral care

Wendy Billington

In every church, of every size, meeting people's pastoral needs is a core area of ministry. If leadership resources are already stretched, however, it can be an area in which it is all too easy to fall short, with potentially disastrous consequences. We may notice and feel compassion when we see somebody struggling in some way, but we also need to be properly equipped in order to offer the kind of wise and practical assistance that will start to guide them back towards wholeness of life.

Earthed in Jesus' command to love one another, this book shows how home groups can be places where people's pain and difficulties are noticed, and first steps taken to help. Wendy Billington offers valuable insights coupled with down-to-earth advice, drawing on her years of pastoral work, as well as on her personal experiences of loss and cancer.

ISBN 978 1 84101 799 0   £6.99
Available from your local Christian bookshop or, in case of difficulty, direct from BRF using the order form on page 207. You may also order from www.brfonline.org.uk.

ORDERFORM

REF	TITLE	PRICE	QTY	TOTAL
876 8	Time for Reflection	£8.99		
878 2	Writing the Icon of the Heart	£6.99		
588 0	The Jesus Prayer	£5.99		
710 5	Seasons of the Spirit	£6.99		
544 6	Working from a Place of Rest	£6.99		
799 0	Growing a Caring Church	£6.99		

POSTAGE AND PACKING CHARGES				
Order value	UK	Europe	Surface	Air Mail
£7.00 & under	£1.25	£3.00	£3.50	£5.50
£7.10–£30.00	£2.25	£5.50	£6.50	£10.00
Over £30.00	FREE	prices on request		

Postage and packing	
Donation	
TOTAL	

Name _____ Account Number _____

Address _____

_____ Postcode _____

Telephone Number_____

Email _____

Payment by: ❑ Cheque ❑ Mastercard ❑ Visa ❑ Postal Order ❑ Maestro

Card no ☐☐☐☐ ☐☐☐☐ ☐☐☐☐ ☐☐☐☐ ☐☐☐

Valid from ☐☐☐☐ Expires ☐☐☐☐ Issue no. ☐☐☐

Security code* ☐☐☐ *Last 3 digits on the reverse of the card. Shaded boxes for
ESSENTIAL IN ORDER TO PROCESS YOUR ORDER Maestro use only

Signature _____ Date _____

All orders must be accompanied by the appropriate payment.

Please send your completed order form to:
BRF, 15 The Chambers, Vineyard, Abingdon OX14 3FE
Tel. 01865 319700 / Fax. 01865 319701 Email: enquiries@brf.org.uk

❑ Please send me further information about BRF publications.

Available from your local Christian bookshop.   BRF is a Registered Charity

About

BRF is a registered charity and also a limited company, and has been in existence since 1922. Through all that we do—producing resources, providing training, working face-to-face with adults and children, and via the web—we work to resource individuals and church communities in their Christian discipleship through the Bible, prayer and worship.

Our Barnabas children's team works with primary schools and churches to help children under 11, and the adults who work with them, to explore Christianity creatively and to bring the Bible alive.

To find out more about BRF and its core activities and ministries, visit:

www.brf.org.uk
www.brfonline.org.uk
www.barnabasinschools.org.uk
www.barnabasinchurches.org.uk
www.messychurch.org.uk
www.foundations21.org.uk

If you have any questions about BRF
and our work, please email us at

enquiries@brf.org.uk